Hope Indeed!

Hope Indeed!

Remarkable Stories of Peacemakers

N. Gerald Shenk

Good Books

Intercourse, PA 17534
800/762-7171
www.GoodBooks.com

Front cover photograph by Carl Hiebert.
Design by Cliff Snyder

HOPE INDEED!
Copyright ©2008 by Good Books, Intercourse, PA 17534
International Standard Book Number: 978-1-56148-632-8
Library of Congress Catalog Card Number: 2008026729

Library of Congress Cataloging-in-Publication Data
Shenk, Gerald, 1953-
  Hope indeed! : remarkable stories of peacemakers / N. Gerald Shenk.
    p. cm.
  ISBN 978-1-56148-632-8 (pbk. : alk. paper) 1. Peace--Religious aspects--
Christianity. I. Title.
  BT736.4.S54 2008
  261.8'730922--dc22   2008026729

TABLE OF CONTENTS

INTRODUCTION

Do we really need more arguments in favor of peace? Before a war is launched, even the generals favor resolving the dispute by other means. Every war is a failure, as any diplomat knows.

But what does it take to get us thinking creatively about alternatives to resolving conflicts through violence? Another fervent speech? More reasoned analysis? An impassioned appeal to our patriotism and our righteous cause?

Somehow, I doubt it. Verbiage is not in short supply.

What we need are stories—evidence of hope from people who faced difficult conflicts with solutions that seem to come from the imagination of God. Some of my favorite thinkers claim that the universe is bent in favor of justice and right relationships. If this is true, and if we can faintly discern it in the record of human history, then there's merit in gathering such hints and clues like the most devoted detectives in the world.

This collection of stories shows how ordinary yet courageous people demonstrated the possibilities of peace in seemingly hopeless circumstances. These stories are their footprints, their road signs for us along the way. In these varied stories, common themes emerge, evidence that something larger than the strength of argument is at work. Faithfulness and integrity *in deeds* shine through the verbiage.

I believe that people of peace need to share their stories boldly. Whenever we are tempted to yield to despair or defeat, these stories can remind us how hope can prevail, hope that does not depend on tanks or full-body armor. I believe we can find the paths that lead to peace, right in the middle of major conflicts. I believe it because I've seen it: brave people who sacrificed security to face down snipers; a Christian relief worker who cared for war victims from "the other side," whose very "betrayals" bore the imprint of Christ's love.

Certainly Christians aren't the only ones qualified to work for peace. This collection honors those peacemakers who consciously act from a framework of faith, and particularly those who identify Christ as their inspiration. From my own experiences in diverse situations, I have found that my beliefs in Christ do not prohibit cooperation with others who believe differently. Indeed, the best stories of other religious traditions converge and resonate with Jesus' call to love our enemies. A couple stories in this collection illustrate this well.

I have been privileged to know and work with a number of the remarkable peacemakers described in these accounts. Nine years of working with churches in socialist Eastern Europe plus many return teaching visits gave me unforgettable stories. Other stories belong to people I haven't met personally but whose stories are available with a bit of research. But all are worth remembering and preserving long after the headlines move on to the next crisis.

I invite you to find your own stories of hope in deeds of courageous peacemaking. Read them. Tell them to your children. Let them percolate throughout your communities. Test them with friends whose circumstances remind you of challenges already faced by other pilgrims on the way. My hope is that all these stories, yours and mine, may inspire a new generation to follow in the footprints of these remarkable peacemakers.

1. CRAZY LIKE JESUS

Lazar was on the eve of being conscripted into one of the world's most notorious armies when I first met him at a youth forum in Serbia convened by his pastor, Alexander. Two years earlier, Alexander had been my student in a Protestant seminary in eastern Croatia during the last days of Tito's Yugoslavia.

As Alexander neared graduation, he called me into his room and earnestly informed me that I had won an argument I didn't even know we were having. "You convinced us to be pacifists," he said.

"But I didn't say anything about pacifism in our classes," I objected. We had studied the New Testament and Christian ethics and some sociology of religion. We stayed with classic Christian topics. I wasn't there to promote an imported ideology that might get people into trouble.

"Oh but we knew what you really believed," he said. "We searched the New Testament to find all the arguments against your position, but we gave up. There just aren't any biblical arguments against your position. So you won! Now we're pacifists, too.

"The problem, you see, is that when we go back to Serbia and let it be known that we're pacifists, we'll never get a job leading congregations there. Nobody will trust us as pastors. So we're going to do just as you did; we won't say a thing about it. We'll just teach and preach the New Testament, and let people figure it out for themselves. We'll get the jobs we've been preparing for, and people will see the pacifist rationale after they study the New Testament with us, just like we did with you." He seemed pleased with the elegant simplicity of his plan.

"But there will come a time when some things need to be said," Alexander continued with a note of urgency in his voice, "and we as local pastors won't be able to say them explicitly. But you'll still be coming back here, you'll be in the area, and we'll give you a call. You can say things as a foreigner that we can't say ourselves. So you'll come when we call. Okay? Deal?"

How could I refuse? These were my students. And I'd never known them to think strongly and passionately about something and hold back from voicing it. When did a boisterous Serb ever not tell you what he's thinking? So I consented, believing this call would never come.

Some two years later, I was teaching again at the same seminary where Alexander and his Serbian partners had studied. The country was days from civil war, which would erupt quickly between Serbia and Croatia. Croatia wanted to opt out of the Yugoslav union to stand alone as an independent state, while

Serbia sought to enforce federal unity. Pastor Alexander was at his home on the Serbian side, and I was just across the line in Croatia, a boundary that would soon become a bloody battleground. Tanks were lined up on the Serbian side, tensely waiting for the Croatian referendum on independence.

It was June 1991. The Croatian side was getting restless; the Serbian side issued blunt warnings. It was hard to teach. Then came the call: "Shenk, we need you to come to Serbia this weekend," Pastor Alexander said. "After the regular Bible study on Saturday evening, our congregation is holding a forum for the youth. The topic is 'Jesus and War—Yes or No?' And you are the speaker! This is it—you remember our deal? You have to come."

Novi Sad in Serbia lay on the next big bend in the Danube, just an hour or two from the seminary in Croatia. A friend and I crossed the lines of tanks waiting for the signal that would come less than two weeks later. When we arrived, we found the Bible study in full tilt. Soon came the end of the service, and the entire congregation stayed for the youth forum. The youth managed to sit in the front rows, at least, but this hot topic had caught the interest of young and old alike.

I tried to present a balanced account of various Christian responses to war throughout the centuries. Some had served gladly in their country's cause; others, reluctantly. Still others had refused. Different denominations had their own traditions of response. Slouching low in the front row, Lazar spoke up. "Look, I'm just a week away from being drafted. That's all well and good, how different Christians have responded. But what would you actually do in my place?"

I answered that I would refuse to serve, and I know that my church would support my decision. But I added, "I don't think it's quite fair to compare our situations. In my society it is a basic human right for someone to object to war and refuse to participate on grounds of religious belief and personal conscience.

"In your situation," I said, "it would be a lot harder to follow my lead without a congregation's backing and without four centuries of experience in paying the price. Anabaptist believers have been following this path together for a long time. That doesn't make it easy or simple, but it would be much harder to do alone."

Lazar thought for a while, and others asked questions. At the end of the evening, Lazar declared that he would try to do what the Protestant pastors and other sincere Christians had done in peacetime under the Communist regime: He would try to be a good soldier and a good Christian at the same time. "Maybe I can be a witness to others that way," he said.

I gave Lazar a blessing and urged him to keep asking himself, "What would Jesus do?"

As I occasionally returned to teach in that area over the next few years, I sometimes heard reports about Lazar. In stray snatches, I pieced together stories that always included a few key elements. He had been ordered into a tank to attack Osijek, a city just across the border from Serbia in Croatia, and he refused. "Jesus won't let me kill," he said. Next the reports suggested a difficult confrontation with a commanding officer, each account concluding with the remark: "Get this guy out of here. He's crazy!"

In the spring of 1993, I returned to Novi Sad with a film crew to document stories of nonviolent responses to the war. Again we found Lazar's pastor, Alexander. The congregation was still meeting under difficult circumstances and still going against the stream of popular culture during those war-crazed years. Alexander arranged to take us to Lazar's workplace where he told his story firsthand. Pastor Alexander conducted the interview.

Lazar recounted in vivid detail the tough exchange he had with his commander on the day his unit was ordered into tanks to attack Osijek, the same town where his pastor, Alexander, had been my student several years earlier. Lazar refused, citing his faith as the reason. Had he claimed a Croatian ethnic heritage, he would have been excused from attacking a Croatian city. Or had he claimed family in Osijek, he may have been excused. But to state simply and calmly that "Jesus will not let me do this" outraged the commander, who brandished his pistol and shouted, "Religion has nothing to do with this. This is war, fellow! I'd rather kill my own father and brother than to let you off like this! And I have the right to kill you for flagrant disobedience to a direct military order."

Lazar calmly acknowledged that he knew he could be killed for this action. "But," he continued, "I know I'll be with Jesus then, and that is more important to me."

The commander stared at Lazar in disbelief. Then he spun around, put the weapon back in his holster, and snapped, "Get this guy out of here! He's crazy."

Lazar then was subjected to testing and maltreatment in what passes for military psychiatric units. Eventually, however, he was returned to his unit in a non-combat role. That's when the tide changed for

Lazar. Until that point, when he had tried to give his faith testimony to others in his unit, they had paid little attention. Now, however, he was respected and treated with dignity. After taking this costly stand, Lazar gained the respect of his chief detractor in his unit. With a smile touched with wonder, Lazar recounted that, rather than ignoring or mocking his Christian witness, his fellow soldiers began to listen to his message, and several of them decided to follow Jesus.

Lazar's congregation had, indeed, found numerous ways to support him during his times of testing. His pastor, Alexander, visited him near the front lines. The congregation carried him in prayer and gave much moral support.

The Serbian army in what was left of the crumbling Yugoslav regime had no policy for dealing with conscientious objection to military service. Thousands of people were scrambling to avoid the long reach of an unwelcome conscription. Some went into hiding. Even overnight on a battlefield, many slipped away undetected, leaving their uniforms behind.

Lazar's bold and costly witness stood out against the silent desertion that thousands of others were choosing. Remarkably, he had managed to return to his unit and find the non-combatant role that accorded with his convictions, while gaining the respect of his comrades. After completing his military term, Lazar returned to civilian life and to his congregation with well-earned confidence. Indeed, being "crazy" seemed to fit the church's calling amid the moral dilemmas of a rogue state in a rogue war.

2. TURNING ENEMIES INTO FRIENDS

A friend from my college days three decades ago walked into my office one January with a story. Ned Wyse and I had crossed paths a number of times in the intervening years but rarely with time for an extended conversation. He was reluctant to impose on my schedule, but I sensed that behind his warm and humble demeanor, a story was aching to be told. And I was eager to listen. After a few pleasantries, Ned said, "It seems that God has really been up to something recently." He began to describe a violent incident he had experienced some five years earlier, with consequences that were still unfolding.

Ned is a farmer and Mennonite pastor in a rural community in lower Michigan. He was driving his pick-up truck near his home one September day in 1999 when several young men he didn't recognize drove past in the opposite direction. He thought they may have been newcomers to the community, so he waved to them, a neighborly custom in his area.

Ned was startled when one of the men in the car made an obscene gesture in reply. Thinking there might be a problem, Ned stopped the truck, hoping to talk things out with them. He remembers thinking, "I need to let them know that this isn't acceptable in this community. If nobody ever addresses such behavior, how will they learn?" The other car also slid to a stop. Within seconds, three youths ran menacingly toward his truck. Before Ned could get out, they pulled a broken piece of fence post from his truck bed and smashed the rear window. One youth ran to the passenger door, but it was locked. Another ran to Ned's open window, shouting obscenities and punching Ned's face. Bleeding profusely and in shock, Ned hit the gas and pulled away. The attackers fled back to their car and sped off. Ned's only visual contact with them had been a glimpse in the rear-view mirror as they approached his truck.

Bewildered and in excruciating pain, Ned drove the last half mile to his home and arrived needing medical attention for a deep cut above his eye. A 911 call alerted the hospital that he had been assaulted and would arrive there shortly. That call eventually brought a sheriff's deputy to the hospital to investigate the attack. "Who had done this?" the officer asked. "Were the attackers known in the community?"

Ned described the car and gave a sketchy description of the three attackers. But he had no idea who they were, nor why they would attack him. The officers had received a report of another unprovoked attack in the vicinity that same day, and Ned's description of the vehicle and of the assailants matched the details in that incident. Ned thought he remembered seeing the assailants' vehicle at a nearby home, but the police investigation found no leads. "You were simply in the wrong place at the wrong time," one of the officers concluded.

The evening of the attack, the local high school football team had a home game. Word of Ned's attack spread quickly, even growing in the retelling. "It reminded me that a crime is never committed against an individual alone," Ned reflected. "It's actually a violation against the whole community."

Not knowing who had attacked him or with what motives, Ned and his family were left to suspect the worst. Was it an old grudge? A reaction to decisions taken earlier while Ned served on the local school board? How could he know the attackers wouldn't come back? "We had never locked our doors before this took place," he recalled wistfully.

The heightened concern took its toll in the wider community as well. Ten days after the attack, a neighbor and his son stopped by to discuss it with Ned. "Just let us know who you think did this, and we'll take care of it. They have to know they can't do stuff like this in our community!"

Ned answered that he didn't think retaliation would solve anything. Furthermore, he still did not know who had done it. As weeks, months, then years passed, the crime remained unsolved and the perpetrators were still at large.

For four long years, Ned went about the tasks of his life without discovering who had attacked him or why. Many times he drove by the house where he thought he might have seen the assailants' car parked. He prayed for an opportunity to know who had attacked him so he might work to undo the damages. But he never saw that car again, and he finally gave up hope of ever knowing what had gone wrong and why.

But then, as Ned described it, "God began putting all these things together" for a possible reconciliation. Near Thanksgiving 2003, a neighbor swung by to ask permission to hunt in a swampy part of Ned's farmland. He wanted to bag some venison for his son, Matt, who was receiving treatments at the University of Michigan hospital for a brain tumor. Ned remembered Matt from some interactions Ned had while serving on the school board.

"Does Matt have any pastoral care?" Ned asked.

The dad said, "No, we don't go to church."

"I'd be glad to go visit Matt," Ned offered. "I'm a minister."

Surprised, the dad readily agreed that Matt would welcome a visit. Within a few days, Ned had traveled to see Matt three times in the hospital and had prayed with him. Ned gave Matt a New Testament after telling a set of Bible stories (one of Ned's passions) from Luke 15—Jesus' parable of the lost coin, the lost sheep, and the lost son. Matt soon began to pray in Ned's presence, vowing to serve God.

Matt was scheduled for surgery later that week, and soon thereafter Ned learned that Matt had been released and was recovering at a friend's home. Hearing the address, Ned recognized it as the same house he had suspected of harboring his assailants some four years earlier. Despite some lurking misgivings, he determined to visit Matt there.

In one of Ned's first visits during Matt's recovery, Matt began discussing his friend, "Tom," who was currently in prison on various charges. "I need some Bible verses for Tom," Matt said. "He's in prison, and he wants to talk with you about an incident that happened on the road a few years ago."

Ned began arranging to visit Tom in jail but discovered that regulations would not allow it. The following Sunday as Matt accompanied Ned to church for the first time, Matt handed Ned a letter from Tom. Hearing of Ned's kindness to Matt during his hospitalization and surgery, Tom wrote a letter that appeared to be spotted with water or tears, asking for Ned's forgiveness for his part in the assault four years earlier.

Three months later, Tom was released from prison and his first order of business was to meet Matt's new friend, Ned. Tom shook Ned's hand, saying, "I'm sorry! We were drinkin' and doin' drugs when it happened."

"You know that doesn't make it okay," Ned responded. "You hurt more than me that day. You really hurt my family, too."

Again, Tom repeated, "I'm just so sorry."

Ned then expressed his forgiveness, and said, "I'd like to know who else I can forgive."

"It was my two brothers," Tom replied, "and my sister was driving the car."

Tom and his fiancée, Marie, were expecting a child, and a few days after their child was born, Ned took a gift to them. This tangible gesture of goodwill seemed to cement the verbal acts of forgiveness.

Later, Ned was asked to help Matt's father with some heavy loading. Tom and his brother, "Ben," were also helping. At one point during the work, Ned asked Ben directly, "Is it okay if I forgive you?"

Ben said, "Yes! Last winter I was stuck in the snow by your house, and you came along to shovel me out. I really appreciated that."

Further opportunity for reconciliation occurred when Marie and Tom were preparing to marry. License in hand, they were headed to see a justice of the peace when Marie suggested asking Ned to marry them instead. In a two-hour conversation with the couple, Ned learned that Marie, too, had been in the car when the assault took place. She recalled that someone in the car thought that Ned had made an obscene gesture instead of the friendly wave.

Two weeks later, Ned married Tom and Marie at Ned's home. In attendance were Tom's parents, a brother, and an aunt. Ned's daughter, who had been traumatized by the attack on her dad, also was present to help with the wedding.

In the view of disbelieving neighbors, the wedding "took the cake." How could you let someone who attacked you come into your own home? they wondered.

After the wedding, Tom and his bride were shopping at a nearby store and the clerk said, "Have a nice day."

"We're having a great day," Tom replied. "We just got married!" Then he told the clerk how the wedding had culminated in a process of reconciliation after an assault. In an ironic twist, the store owner's family members were among those who had offered to retaliate after the attack.

The story gained momentum as more neighbors began to hear of the concrete steps Ned took toward forgiveness and restoration. A local Christian business owner who had often heard Ned preach as a guest at his church expressed surprise that Ned had invited the offenders into his home. Ned replied, "Well, when Jesus said to love your enemies, I don't think he was kidding."

A sad chapter in the story occurred in September 2005 when Matt's dad was accidentally shot and killed while hunting. Matt asked Ned to lead the funeral service. During these events, another of Tom's brothers came home and eagerly offered Ned a prompt and direct apology. "I'm so sorry for the (crap) we did to you on the road," he said. Again, Ned affirmed God's love for him.

This encounter with the final assailant completed the process of repentance and reconciliation for the damages done in the original attack. The story could have ended there, but Ned continued to build relationships with various members of the two extended and troubled family systems. One of the repentant brothers successfully completed three months in an Alcoholics Anonymous program, which helped to restore his relationship with his wife and gain back his job. Then came the news about a half year later that this brother and his wife, who lived about an hour away from Ned, had been baptized in a local church. Later, Tom and Marie also were baptized and joined a local church.

As Ned recounted these experiences, he conceded that each reconciling conversation had been difficult for himself and for his attackers. The emotional trauma and physical damage that Ned and his family experienced had been severe. This was evident as he sat in my office telling the story. The wounds were so fresh it seemed almost disrespectful to probe the details of who said what in each exchange. But I wondered, How does a victim receive such confessions? And is it wise to pursue reconciliation without a public framework to guarantee justice and balance out claims for injury and loss?

The decision to forgo retaliation had been costly for Ned, and especially for his family members. The cost multiplied over years of not knowing who was behind the random attack. Yet Ned's attackers and his would-be avengers benefited from his patience. As the process of transformation unfolded in the wider neighborhood, Ned's story became a local parable of repaying evil with good. Two of Ned's neighbors were drawn to join his congregation because of the way he had responded when he was attacked.

Soon after Tom and Marie's wedding, Ned received a note from Tom's aunt, who wrote:

Thank you for your hospitality in Thomas & Marie's wedding. The fact that you opened your home to them after what was done to you did make an impact on so many in our family. The conversation has come up many times and has helped to correct the way some of the young ones were looking at Christians. So many times they only see hypocrites but you have truly turned the other cheek and they saw that example! Seeing Jesus in you may be the only time many of these young people ever meet Him.

God's Peace and Love to You.

I have seen photos of Ned's face after the brutal beating and of his battered truck. He easily might have sought revenge, but instead he showed extraordinary strength of character to befriend his "enemies" with ordinary acts of human kindness. Certainly, making things right requires tremendous imagination and fortitude of spirit—but the fruits are lasting and sweet.

3. A FRANCISCAN IN THE FRAY

The Franciscan order in Bosnia has a long history of staying with their people during times of struggle. During the medieval period, the Turks came sweeping to power in the Balkans and installed Islamic rule for 500 years. Even though the regular parish priests fled, the Franciscans remained to share the fate of ordinary folk.

In the deeper roots of Franciscan history is a charming account of Brother Francis, who traveled with Christian crusaders to Egypt to preach love for one's enemies and laying down one's weapons. Francis determined to meet the Sultan, the Muslim ruler, and from that meeting, both the Sultan and Brother Francis gained new respect for the other.[1]

The Franciscans held a significant role in society, even during Yugoslavia's religiously restrictive period of communist rule. They promoted substantial biblical scholarship and confidently engaged in dialogue with the authorities, which drew respect from all sides in the ethnically diverse region. The Franciscans seemed to view the entire population as their own—those affiliated with the Catholic church, with the Orthodox, with Islam, or those with no religious ties whatsoever. And that loyalty was reciprocated.

Brother Ivo Marković, a priest in his twenties, was active in a rural region during the late 1970s. He was training young seminarians in the skills needed for ministry. His special passion was music, and "Fra Ivo" ("Fra" comes from the Latin *frater,* meaning "brother"), was never more at home than in the midst of a choir.

Little more than a decade later, however, Bosnia had become a society unraveled by genocide; torture camps; cities under siege for months; and civilian populations trapped without food, shelter, or medical care. Neighbors turned against each other, and the whole region spiraled into ethnic fear and hatred, right in the middle of modern Europe. President Tito's maverick 50-year experiment with communism in a multi-ethnic society had failed. Yugoslavia was breaking up, sending streams of refugees into surrounding countries. The international system was stymied. For more than four years (1991-95), interventions were feeble and ineffective.

Fra Ivo made it his job to resist the fear and communal violence in his beloved Bosnia. When tensions flared up at the village level, he would cross over into "enemy" territory and, in one-on-one interactions, insist that all of Bosnia's people belonged to each other. Even as the different ethnic groups pulled apart and took shelter in separate enclaves, he brought people together to talk about the neighbors and neighborhoods they once shared.

I learned of Fra Ivo's story around 1992 when mutual friends pointed me toward his work for peace in central Bosnia. He had been forced at gunpoint into exile from Sarajevo, Bosnia's capital, when his seminary there was overrun by Serbian forces. Having faced down death on numerous occasions, Fra Ivo was again receiving death threats even from forces on his own side, some Croatian partisans.

Fra Ivo advocated boldly for a Bosnia that would guarantee safety for all its constituent groups (primarily Bošnjak-Muslim, Serbian, and Croatian). He insisted that Bosnia isn't Bosnia if it's carved into separate ethnic enclaves, as international negotiators Cyrus Vance and Lord Carrington were proposing. Although some in his own Catholic circles called for separatist solutions to the strife, Fra Ivo remained adamant that Bosnia belongs to all Bosnians. In every opportunity, he persisted in relating across the divides with constant reminders of the life that Bosnians shared *together.*

In 1993, while the fighting raged in Bosnia, Fra Ivo participated in a group of peacemakers who gathered in Austria from embattled Bosnia, Serbia, and Croatia. At that gathering, Fra Ivo told of tough encounters he'd had, right in the thick of the fighting. Once he had entered a village to rescue a young girl who was being held in a house at gunpoint. He determined to confront the armed guards directly. When they threatened him with a bayonet, he got angry and declared that he wasn't there to hurt anyone. How could they use weapons against a priest? "If you're going to kill me, then kill me right now!" he protested. They backed down and released the girl. It was not the first time that death threats failed to deter Fra Ivo. And it certainly was not the last.

Fra Ivo also described how he defied widespread suspicion and fear by visiting the other side during a season of relative calm. He used a cease-fire to travel to Serb-held territories outside besieged Sarajevo. Going into the surrounding hills, he initiated conversations in outlying villages among refugees and displaced persons. In a low-key manner, he invited people to reflect on the way things used to be just a few months earlier when they had lived with their neighbors in peace. "Where did you live?" he would ask. "Who were your neighbors (the other ethnic groups) there? Did you have difficulties with each other? How did you get along despite the differences back then?"

These conversations took place under the watch of nervous soldiers, whose main task was keeping ethnic groups apart. "Ah yes, we had good neighbors; we got together for each other's festivals and religious holidays. We shared the fruits of our gardens; we watched each other's children. We knew how to live a good life together back there."

In resurrecting these happier memories, the sad shape of the present shattering violence loomed large. More recent memories seemed to overshadow the happier ones, memories of sudden fear and suspicion, reports of atrocities far away that made trusting one's neighbors seem foolish. Rumors spread like fire in a dry forest. The instinct to follow the crowd is proverbial in the region–"Wherever all the Turks go, there goes little Muhammad also."

As suspicion escalated about Fra Ivo's activities, he eventually was banned from visiting the displaced people in the hills surrounding his besieged Sarajevo. The soldiers determined that his innocent chatting over coffee about the way things used to be was not at all harmless. "You remind people of what they had before things split up," they told him. "We know your strategy; you are stirring up dangerous memories."

And that, indeed, was exactly Fra Ivo's intention: to stir up the dangerous memories of peace and neighborly co-existence. It was his trademark priestly subversion.

But the militias on the other side weren't the only ones trying to tamp down Fra Ivo's subversion. Armed forces on his own side were threatening the custodians of Christian faith among the people. For instance, they tried to forbid them from holding Mass, saying, "The Eucharist is not effective among the people during a time of war." Fra Ivo and his fellow priests used the Mass to teach people about forgiveness and love toward one's enemies. The old rituals had some power left in them after all!

The toughest trials for Fra Ivo came during the middle of the four-year war in Bosnia. He had returned home to his parents' village in central Bosnia. A sudden shift in the tides of war pitted two former allies against each other: Croats and Bosnian Muslims became opponents almost overnight. For the first two years, these two groups fought against renegade Serbs, but suddenly the fight developed three distinct battle fronts. It was widely reported that foreign volunteers were augmenting the beleaguered Muslims at the center of the fray. Known as the *mujahedin,* these foreigners cared little for the history of alliances and goodwill that marked neighborly relations at the local level.

Fra Ivo's extended family lived in a Croat Catholic village adjacent to a Muslim village, and the two communities had preserved good relationships to that point. Then, in the spring of 1992, rumors circulated of tensions and atrocities committed between the groups in other regions. The locals started throwing up defenses against each other, digging trenches, and forbidding passage. Overnight, the former allies became fearfully suspicious of each other.

Fra Ivo would have none of this. Grabbing his habit, the distinctive brown cloak that marks Franciscans all over Bosnia, he headed for the new border between the two villages. First his own side's militia tried to stop him. Then the Muslim recruits in the trenches warned, "Stop! Or we'll shoot!"

Fra Ivo says, "Then I got angry. I went right toward them. I said, 'You can see I'm here as a Franciscan, not as a soldier. If you're going to shoot me, then shoot!' But they calmed down and let me approach. I told them I wanted to talk to the religious leader on their side so we can work things out. The guards led me to a café, and the *hodža* came out to meet me. He was so pleased to see me. We sat and talked, and then we got the militia leaders from both sides to talk. Right there we agreed to a cease-fire and joint patrols. We started a true 'peace process' that lasted for a whole year."

Even while Croats and Muslims all around them in central Bosnia engaged in sporadic fighting, these locals managed to stave off the hatred and mistrust by joint efforts that assured each other's security. "If someone from our side targets you, we will protect you," they vowed to each other. "They will have to take us first."

And that's the way it worked for a full year, Fra Ivo said. Later, however, atrocities elsewhere sparked such a vicious reaction that outside forces, including the foreign *mujahedin*, rampaged through this calmer region. These radicalized Muslims who had no neighborly connection with the local communities first disarmed the local Muslims and then ripped through the quiet Croat community.

Fra Ivo and I were traveling together that day in a small car in neighboring Croatia. We were headed for his seminary-in-exile, where I was invited to give a lecture on New Testament understandings of non-violence. Reports of violence in his home community came across the radio news. Hearing the location of the current fighting, Fra Ivo knew that his family was facing severe hardship. Several days later, he learned that his father and at least a dozen of his extended family were killed in that violence.

Their deaths, however, would not deter Fra Ivo. Even in grief, he declared, "If there is just one Muslim on the other side still working for peace, I will keep on also."

Fra Ivo's mission to mend the torn fabric of Bosnian society continues as a consuming passion even today. Within a short period after open warfare ended in Bosnia, he had returned to pick up the pieces. He convened a singing group from the constituent groups of Bosnia. Serbs, Croats, Muslims, Jews, and Marxists came together to learn and perform the sacred music from each other's traditions. By demonstrating appreciation for each heritage in public performances, their work helped to rebuild the bridges and ties that formerly held Bosnia together. The choir, named "Pontanima," meaning "soul bridge," has won several international awards and still tours extensively within the region.

Fra Ivo has gained recognition and some notoriety as a representative of the living hope that Bosnia's suffering people can come back together for the good of all. Much international and local effort has been spent to reduce the violence and restore the infrastructure. But the tasks of healing and recovery from traumas will continue for many, many years.

As I watched Fra Ivo in 1993 receive the grievous news that violence had decimated his own family, I saw his spirit struggling to survive. He was struggling to restore his own confidence and hope that the human community could cherish differences and uphold dignity for all. When Fra Ivo and his fellow priests persisted in celebrating the Eucharist during the war, especially when it was deemed "counter-productive" for war efforts, they demonstrated the mystery of Christ's love in life and death for all humanity.

Fra Ivo was not the only Franciscan in Bosnia and Croatia working for peace. His witness, and those of other Franciscans, is a triumph over mercenary and fanatical violence in a time of war. Fra Ivo's life is a testament of faith that you can face thugs and rebels, mercenaries and *mujahedin*, without caving in to despair, hatred, or vengeance when you are animated by the gospel of peace.

4. Moving Toward the Trouble

For many Americans, the 1992 Los Angeles riots seared into memory a series of violent images. The story began in March 1991 when Rodney King, an African American, was stopped along a freeway by police for traffic violations. Four police officers were caught on videotape, beating King and repeatedly shoving him to the ground.

The four officers charged with the beating (three white and one Hispanic) were brought to trial in a process that ended more than a year later. Tensions skyrocketed across Los Angeles as the outcome hung in the balance. Then on April 29, 1992, all hell broke loose in South Central Los Angeles moments after the jury acquitted the four officers of the key charges. Violence erupted in the streets. Rage boiled over at a system that seemed so blatantly unjust and racist. Angry youths set buildings on fire and looted stores. Roving gangs pillaged shops, unchecked by security forces that appeared only to protect firefighters at select locations.

Some also remember Rodney King's plea as he watched the mayhem: "Can we all get along?" Many agreed and wondered where all this rage came from. Most of the time, our civil society appears reasonably calm on the surface. Could there really be so much intense heat smoldering beneath the surface that the moment a verdict is announced, a volcano of aggrieved resentment and hatred erupts? It took such an eruption to remind Americans with stinging ferocity how entrenched racism is in our communities.

For a long time I had wondered how to deal constructively with the realities of racial tensions and historic injustices. Conventional wisdom advises us to keep our heads down, stay away from troubled zones and, if we can help it, stay out of disputes that are not our own. For most citizens in many parts of the country, these maxims keep us well removed from civil disturbances.

My own upbringing in a largely Mennonite, rural community provided another lens through which to view social tensions. Immersed in a strong and separate faith identity, I felt relatively safe. The faith my community emphasized taught me to turn away from violence and to stay away from places where violence was likely to erupt. I grew up hearing many stories of people who had gone to great lengths to avoid inflicting violence of any kind.

As a teenager during the restless end of the 1960s, a sizeable stretch of imagination (and plenty of newspapers) brought me a hint of the frustration and alienation my urban peers were facing. We looked with suspicion at those who joined anti-war demonstrations and civil rights marches. That sort of activism didn't fit us either. We were taught in many subtle ways to avoid conflict, to do all in our power not to actively confront another. I saw and heard repeatedly that we are people who keep to ourselves. We let others do whatever they think they must to resolve the tough problems.

Ironically, this withdrawn, passive approach to the world's conflicts didn't square with our own historical faith. Separatist Mennonites are heirs of Anabaptist ancestors who stood up to unjust authorities even when threatened with torture and death. Our ancestors spoke out in the public square for fairness and justice in the name of Christ. And as I moved beyond the quietude of my rural community into broader circles of Mennonites, I discovered many who, while refraining from war and violence, actively addressed pressing social problems. Many modern Mennonites moved toward the world's suffering, and they became my models. Indeed, for much of the 20th century, organized groups of Mennonites had been cultivating an energetic humanitarian response to famine, disaster, and urgent development needs around the world.

Against this personal backdrop of separatist passivism and awakened activism, I watched the drama in South Central Los Angeles unfold. The courageous response of four individuals during the riots still stuns me. Despite all my shaping in caution, I'm challenged by those whose faith drew them *toward* trouble, and I hope that I now would respond with similar courage.

As the mob of enraged youths rampaged through the Los Angeles streets, it unleashed its fury on a white truck driver named Reginald Denny. He'd driven unknowingly into the middle of the violence at the intersection of Florence and Normandie. The youths dragged Denny from his truck. In an ironic twist, like Rodney King's beating caught on videotape, this incident was broadcast live on the news from helicopters hovering overhead. In full view of a national audience, the youths bashed Denny's head onto the pavement. They knocked him unconscious, inflicting 91 skull fractures as they pummeled his almost lifeless body.

Four separate individuals watching the events on television just blocks away saw the deadly drama unfolding. Each one said, "I must go help." One was Bobby Green, a truck driver who rushed to the scene. There Green found another rescuer, Lei Yuille, already helping Denny off the street. Together with two other rescuers, Titus Murphy and Terri Barnett, they lifted Denny back into his truck and drove him to a hospital. All four rescuers were African American. Unarmed and unprotected, they moved directly into the zone of greatest danger and, together, saved a white victim from certain death on the street. Later, when reporters tracked down Denny's rescuers, these four individuals brushed aside their status as heroes.

Ten years after the riots, I heard a public radio interview with Lei Yuille. She recounted how the violence had erupted that day and how she had watched the terrifying scenes unfold on the television. As the mob tore into Denny, she recalled saying to her brother, "We're Christians—we need to go and help!"

In her mind, it was that simple. Christians are called to *go*.

5. SHELTERING FALLEN TYRANTS

This story almost got lost amid the swirl of exhilaration and suspicions that swept across newly reunited Germany after the Berlin Wall came down late in 1989. Few parts of communist Eastern Europe had been bleaker than socialist East Germany under the ruthless regime of Erich Honecker.

The grim and deadly Wall that divided Berlin for 28 years was almost synonymous with Honecker's political career as the general secretary of East Germany's ruling Communist party. He had been its chief of state from 1971 until 1989 and had been obsessed with state security even before reaching the highest offices. But when the Wall came down in November 1989, so did his repressive regime. And so did Honecker. The tyrant would soon face criminal charges for the deaths of 192 civilians killed while trying to cross the Berlin Wall during his reign.

My own memory of the Berlin Wall came back to me quite forcefully when its momentous removal transfixed the world in the fall of 1989. During a brief visit to Berlin in 1983 with my family of four, our then four-year-old son was struck with the bristling weaponry and razor-wire fencing as we passed through checkpoints by bus from East Berlin to our destination with church-worker colleagues in West Berlin.

"Why do they have all these guns and fences, Dad?" he asked. I struggled to explain them without legitimizing the fearsome display. "The guns are here because people feel afraid and insecure," I said. "But remember: People put all these walls here, and someday people could take them down."

Raising my children in the late throes of the Cold War, I did not want to endorse the climate of fear that had shaped international relations for my entire lifetime. It would have been electrifying to know then that the menacing Berlin Wall and the whole structure of East-West conflicts would be removed in such a dramatic and almost bloodless fashion by nonviolent popular uprisings just six years later.

When the Berlin Wall came down, Honecker went from dictator to homeless persona non grata within a few short weeks. He was turned out of the presidential villa with his wife, Margot, the former minister for national education. His illness with liver disease gained him a brief stay in a Soviet military hospital. But upon release, he literally had nowhere to go.

A Lutheran pastor, Uwe Holmer, decided to take the homeless Honeckers into his own home, a parsonage in an East Berlin suburb. Aging, ailing, and destitute, the former ruling duo had little help from their long-time comrades in the political elite. Most of their recent communist co-workers and friends were scrambling to distance themselves from the Honeckers.

The Honeckers' legacy in socialist East Germany included notorious repression of human rights. Endless spying by citizens on other citizens created a deep and devastating mistrust toward everyone. One's own spouse or children might covertly be reporting suspicious behavior to the authorities. East Germany had managed to survive the constant pressure of its free and noisy neighbor, West Germany. They did this only by means of relentless vigilance, high walls, firing squads at the border crossings, and ideological repression. Substantial economic and military subsidies from the Soviet Union kept the project afloat.

No independent social structures had survived in East Germany to challenge the severe socialist regime from within. The only part of society where even a small measure of autonomy persisted was the churches. Yet everyone knew the churches also were riddled with secret informants from top to bottom.

Pastor Holmer's own children had paid the price of Honecker's repression in the school system. On eight different occasions they were denied entrance to university studies under rules and restrictions imposed by Honecker's wife in the education ministry. Reasons for rejection were not formally provided; having a pastor for a parent was the only apparent explanation.

Even so, when the former dictator and his wife found themselves homeless, Pastor Holmer invited them into his home and gave them his grown children's rooms. This act of hospitality brought a deluge of criticism and threats from outraged Germans.

Parishioners threatened to leave the church. Contributions dwindled. Hateful letters poured in by the hundreds. People made irate calls to the Holmers. Throngs of protesters filled the small street outside the pastor's home, and local police said they couldn't guarantee safety for the pastor and his family.

Yet Pastor Holmer persisted, extending compassion and hospitality to the fallen leader who was nearly incapacitated by his serious illness. For more than two months in early 1990, the deposed guests joined the Holmers for meals around the table. They participated silently in the table blessing. The compassion they received made sense only in the context of Christ's teaching to love one's enemies. In a letter to the local newspaper editor, Holmer wrote: "In recent days it has become apparent to me in a new way how much it cost God to forgive my sins. ... We want to live by Christ's example."

After several months as the pastor's guests, the Honeckers fled to the Soviet Union in 1991. After that regime also collapsed, the Honeckers were extradited back to Germany in 1992 for trial on the earlier charges. Because of his ill health, however, Honecker was excused from standing trial. Granted exile in Chile in 1993, he died of cancer in May 1994. Ten years after Honecker's death, Pastor Holmer was still advocating for dignity on behalf of the fallen dictator. In a letter to the editor, he called for "a dignified, secure final resting place" for Honecker's ashes in his homeland, if his family so desired.

In 1990, at the height of Pastor Holmer's unpopular hospitality to the Honeckers, he wrote to his local newspaper: "In Lobetal there is a sculpture of Jesus inviting people to himself and crying out, 'Come unto me, all ye that labor and are heavy laden, and I will give you rest.' We have been commanded by our Lord Jesus to follow him and to receive all those who are weary and heavy laden, in spirit and in body, but especially the homeless. ... What Jesus asked his disciples to do is equally binding on us."

The nonviolent revolution that overthrew a hated regime in East Germany in 1989 was inspired by many small and local acts of courage and faith. These acts continued after the regime's fall as Christians and other people of integrity helped to recover a civil society after decades of dehumanizing oppression. Certainly the temptation to seek revenge is powerful—even understandable. But Pastor Holmer's courageous example short-circuited the cycle of violence and retaliation. He gallantly demonstrated how to strive for basic human dignity even on behalf of its chief offenders.

6. A Protest in Generosity

A captain of the poultry industry came to the local Eastern Mennonite High School in Virginia to speak in the morning chapel service. The poultry industry is a vital component in the strong economy of the Shenandoah Valley at the western edge of Virginia. This businessman had been the featured speaker for the business community at the downtown prayer breakfast in Harrisonburg, so someone from the school's chapel planning committee figured that the guest for the prayer breakfast might also do well speaking to high school students.

The speaker enthusiastically shared his personal story as a successful businessman. He credited his personal achievements in the poultry industry to the virtues of honesty, hard work in a market economy, and the importance of Christian faith in his life. His rousing speech reached a climax of patriotic fervor that concluded with a video clip of American flags.

This largely Mennonite audience of teachers and students sat in awkward silence. Mennonites' pacifist heritage is rooted in an allegiance to God above country, making them generally cautious about expressing patriotism. Never had one of their chapel services so unabashedly married Christian faith and nationalist fervor. Making the situation more perplexing, the speaker gave each person in the audience a $20 bill tucked inside an evangelistic tract that reinforced his values of hard work, American markets, and Christian faith. After his address, the speaker left promptly.

Now what? Students and teachers filed out of the auditorium toward their first classes. No one could quite believe what had happened. Various teachers, sensing the unease, took time in their classes to process the chapel service. The speaker's story was a fascinating account of how a person can achieve significant success in today's complex globalizing economy. It was worth reflecting on. Several of the students and their families were employed in the poultry industry. At the very least, the faculty and students owed common courtesy to the guest who had shared his story as a Christian businessman in their chapel service.

The teachers used this opportunity to discuss with students how well personal piety and patriotic fervor mesh. They discussed the difference between the reign of God and the reign of Western consumerism that often typifies the American way of life.

Some of the students began wondering what to do with the $20 bill they were given. At $20 each, the businessman had laid out some $6,000 that morning at the high school. Some chose to pocket the money, delighted at the unexpected generosity. But others hesitated. They discussed whether accepting the gift might make them complicit in a method and a message that had stirred much ambivalence and critique. So they faced a dilemma. If they kept the $20, did they have a right to criticize the presentation for mixing piety and patriotic fervor? If they rejected that message, could they find a way to make a different statement without being discourteous to their guest?

Then, two students, including our freshman daughter, Greta, hit on an idea. What if they found a worthy project to which everyone could contribute instead? They began researching giving projects on the Internet and settled on the Heifer Project International, a program that gives agricultural and development aid to people living in poverty around the world. Quickly the girls put their alternate proposal together.

With approval from school staff, they set up a table in a busy hallway near the cafeteria and distributed information about how students' contributions could make a difference for people in need. The pitch was simple: Would you consider contributing money to the Heifer Project to help others? Suggested amount: $20!

Not everyone parted with their windfall profits that day. But students, faculty, and staff together contributed more than $1,200 to Heifer Project International that week to purchase a menagerie of animals, including a water buffalo and two goats.

Greta came home that evening saying it had been her best day ever in high school. She felt exhilarated that the students had found a way to turn an awkward situation into a marvelous opportunity to help people in need.

As a parent, I was grateful that teachers had created space for discussion and then encouraged an active, creative response. And I was proud of our daughter who, with Thea Litchfield, was a sparkplug for the project. They and 60 fellow students, faculty, and staff together multiplied a few $20 bills into a magnanimous gesture of goodwill.

7. PEACEMAKING ON AN INTERNATIONAL ORDER

Sometimes we seem to think that peace, like war, is the primary domain of nation states. Since only nations can wage war, the reasoning goes, then the agents of nations, diplomats, must be the sole representatives for negotiating peace.

If war and peace belong to the realm of nations, then what impact can amateurs and novices have for peace? Is there room on the big stage of world events for small actors in supporting roles? Or are they simply the understudies, waiting to take on the larger roles if the main characters somehow lapse?

Conventional wisdom is shifting significantly in recent years. Indeed, a growing body of evidence supports the legitimacy and effectiveness of non-state actors in seeking peace among conflicted parties. This is the premise, in part, of Track Two diplomacy. Many peacebuilding tasks cannot be pursued in the full light of public scrutiny. Behind the scenes, numerous activists quietly prepare the way for the signing of peace agreements under the glare of spotlights.

Andrea Bartoli is one such non-state actor committed to working behind the scenes in Track Two diplomacy. He is a member of a Christian community that had its small beginnings 40 years ago in Rome, Italy, but since has become quite prominent in peacemaking circles for its effective work in large-scale conflicts. The community came to be called Sant'Egidio, named for the high school where its members started meeting in 1968. In that season of widespread student unrest and open rebellion, these young Christians came together to engage in a ministry of social transformation. They wanted to bring the truth of the gospel to bear on public concerns.

I had met Andrea after he reported to an attentive audience of religious-based peace activists in Sweden in 2004. Over coffee, he shared that, after four decades, the community had become a significant advocate for social welfare in Rome and elsewhere. They address the needs of children at risk, the homeless, immigrants, the elderly, orphans, and people dealing with HIV/AIDS. They now number some 300 groups in many cities of Italy and a wider membership of 10,000 around the globe. Andrea himself currently teaches in New York.

In 1986 Pope John Paul II recognized the Sant'Egidio group for its Christian witness to people on the social margins. He commended their spirit of openness to engage in dialogue with people of other religions and their tasks of service among the world's poor.

The regular activities of the Sant'Egidio community in Rome include friendship with international students. This is how a young priest from Mozambique, Don Jaime Goncalves, first came into the community's orbit in 1976. The members' relationship with Goncalves launched a lengthy chapter of the Sant'Egidio community's work in Mozambique, in southern Africa. Long held as a Portuguese colony, it had gained independence abruptly in 1975 after more than a decade of armed insurgency and struggle toward liberation. The FRELIMO party gained power, and its leader, Samora Machel, took office as the new country's first president with an explicitly anti-religious socialist ideology.

The first five years of independence were marked by white flight; nationalization of property and industry; and destabilizing attacks by its nearest neighbors, white-ruled Rhodesia and South Africa. The Soviet Union and Cuba embraced the socialist experiment with substantial foreign aid. A similar war for liberation in next-door Rhodesia culminated in a newly independent Zimbabwe in 1980.

Drastic policy failures combined with drought produced widespread starvation and desperation in Mozambique during the early 1980s. Another resistance movement (RENAMO) formed with outside help in 1977 and in a few short years was stirring up considerable civil unrest and mayhem. The prevailing winds of the Cold War put anti-communist force in the movement's sails.

When the young priest, Goncalves, returned to his homeland after his studies in Rome, he was soon appointed archbishop in a central diocese (Beira). Upon returning to Rome for a synod a year later, he recounted to his Sant'Egidio friends the onerous restrictions that Machel's socialist regime was imposing on Catholic churches. Properties had been confiscated, schools and clinics closed, and Goncalves himself had been imprisoned for half a year.

By then, ironically, the radical Sant'Egidio Christian activists in Rome had fairly congenial ties with their own local communists. They brought the Mozambique archbishop into conversation with these Italian communist leaders, eventually meeting with the chief Italian communist, Enrico Berlinguer, in 1981. The Italian communists began using their own ties to the regime in Mozambique to persuade the new-fledged African communists to relax their restrictions on the practice of religion.

Members of the Sant'Egidio Christian community began visiting Mozambique in 1984, providing food and medicines for humanitarian relief. One shipment in 1985 sent 3,500 tons of aid; another in 1988 delivered 7,000 tons. These relief efforts had the cooperation of Italian diplomatic authorities as well. Some of the aid was sent into rebel-held territories, and Sant'Egidio reps began building trust with the RENAMO insurgents as well.

In the meantime, President Machel's government began to signal a shift away from its hard-line ideology, turning instead toward a more pragmatic approach of solving the urgent problems of hunger and economic collapse. The government began seeking assistance

beyond the socialist camp. Having accumulated insur-
mountable burdens of international debt, the country's productivity had been decimated. Machel flew
to Washington to meet U.S. President Reagan in 1985,
and stopped in Rome on his return to visit with the
pope, a meeting facilitated by the Sant'Egidio community. Machel's death in a 1986 plane crash paved the
way for an even more pragmatic successor in Joaquim
Chissano, who inherited all the failed policies and the
civil war, plus the drought and desperate poverty of
the general population.

By 1989, both of the primary parties to the conflict
in Mozambique (RENAMO and the ruling FRELIMO)
were exhausted. Their outside Soviet patrons were no
longer interested in prolonging the costly support that
had kept a civil war going for almost 15 years. The
diplomats of nearby Zimbabwe, Tanzania, and white-
ruled South Africa were urging compromise and talks
toward resolution.

Each side indicated interest in negotiations but vig-
orously disputed the framework and structure for dialogue. RENAMO, the insurgents, hoped to engage the
West as brokers for a peace process. FRELIMO and
the government insisted on stand-alone talks without
outside facilitation. Each party mistrusted any allies
that the other might bring to the table. Nearby states
were too involved in their surreptitious support, which
had sustained the conflict for more than a decade, to
take a neutral role.

After a variety of false starts and missed appoint-
ments by one side or the other, a coalition of non-state
actors finally brought the parties together in 1990 to
engage in a series of talks that eventually produced a

historic agreement more than two years later. It was the church activists who played a critical role. Only they commanded enough respect and trust on both embattled sides to initiate the dialogue. And at the center of the story was the small Christian community in Rome that had facilitated the meeting between the pope and President Machel when Machel was turning toward pragmatic solutions.

Sant'Egidio and their Mozambiquan allies had gained confidence on all sides with their practical solidarity in humanitarian relief. They had already negotiated with the rebels to secure release of captive priests and nuns. They had blunted the early crude Marxist restrictions on religion. And they had cultivated a wide network of relationships with other formal actors in the diplomatic corps who assisted in crucial moments to facilitate technical aspects of the negotiations.

The critical team of observers in the first rounds of formal talks between RENAMO and FRELIMO included an Italian member of parliament, Goncalves, the archbishop from Mozambique, and two core members of Sant'Egidio. These first steps led to an agreement signed in 1992. Throughout the process, observers secured agreements for continued talks (time and place), set the agenda, and developed the key points of the agreement ultimately reached.

The two sides eventually agreed to provide safe areas for humanitarian relief and to withdraw their combatants to allow desperately needed supplies to reach the beleaguered population. Before this chapter concluded with the official signing in October 1992, the cast of players grew to include the United Nations and official diplomats from numerous countries.

But the key roles in the opening acts and behind the scenes throughout the drama were played by the Christian activists of Sant'Egidio. Their example of quiet and effective persistence lead the way every time we are tempted to ask in the face of massive and intractable conflicts, "But what can one person or even one small community really do about this?"

If we band together in prayerful communities committed to engaging the world with the gospel, there is much we can do.

8. FROM KLAN TO KIN

One of my tests for a good story is whether it grips my imagination and moves me beyond customary thought patterns, whether it exposes a new solution to an old problem. Every now and then a story draws me with wild hope that something special is at work.

In Berlin on a peace study tour in 1984, one story caught my imagination. I heard that a local group of peace activists were going out of their way to attend skinhead rallies—not for confrontation or counter-demonstrations, but to gain insight into the conditions that produced such angry youth. The folks at Reconciliation Action (*Aktion Sühnezeichen*) found that unemployment and deep economic disappointment boiled over into rage at foreigners, immigrants, and others near the bottom of the social ladder. Frustrated hope for a fair share of economic opportunity was moving some at the margins into anti-social behavior.

The finding made plenty of sense. But what I found surprising was the peacemakers' simple yet radical decision to listen to these violent people. Why would this not occur to the rest of us? Our instincts tell us to avoid them. But when folks from Reconciliation Action showed friendship and extended opportunities to them, some of the skinheads left their destructive behaviors.

Is it naïve to think this story is little more than a remarkable aberration? Perhaps. Many people trapped in socially harmful patterns don't readily change their ways. But if we hope to be effective agents of change, we must hold onto the possibility of transformation, even in the most unlikely cases. And that is why a story out of Nebraska captured my imagination when it made national news.

Larry Trapp had a lengthy career in white supremacist movements. Long before 1991, when this story made headlines, he had studied survivalist tactics, dug a bomb shelter, and practiced making explosive devices. In addition, he had accumulated a large trove of hate-filled books, tracts, and propaganda from Hitler's Nazi movement. Having been a police officer for two years in the early 1970s, he possessed a variety of weapons.

In 1988 Trapp joined the Ku Klux Klan, becoming its most visible leader in Nebraska. He set about drawing recruits into the Klan's activities. Together, he and his recruits targeted outspoken black leaders, prominent feminists, immigrants, and homosexual organizations for hostile treatment. They used an arsenal of posters, brochures, threatening packages in the mail, and threatening phone messages.

Though chronic diabetic illness had greatly reduced his mobility and vision, Trapp managed to inflict substantial harm with the help of his youthful followers and to cultivate an aggressive presence, even though confined to a wheelchair. Anyone he perceived as a threat to his movement became a target. African-American homes were fire-bombed, and a Vietnamese cultural center in Omaha was demolished by a gang of neo-Nazi skinheads. Police investigated these and as many as 40 other criminal acts, including numerous fires of suspicious origin, but they were unable to directly tie these acts to Trapp.

When Trapp singled out another set of intended victims in 1991, he set off a series of responses that defied the imaginations of many. One of two synagogues serving the small Jewish community in Lincoln had recently hired a new cantor as its spiritual leader. Cantor Michael Weisser and his family moved into a home they had purchased, glad to settle into their new life.

And then the phone rang. A venomous voice on the other end warned, "You will be sorry you ever moved into 5810 Randolph Street, Jew boy."

Shocked and dismayed, the Weisser family grappled with this hideous threat. Someone not only knew their phone number and address but clearly was bent on intimidation. Soon several packages of vicious and crude propaganda arrived in their mailbox.

Kathryn Watterson describes the drama in her book, *Not By the Sword: How a Cantor and His Family Transformed a Klansman.*[2] Michael, his wife Julie, and their teenage children went through several stages of fear. They felt outraged that such a state of siege could overtake their personal lives. They bought extra locks, monitored their surroundings, secured their home and vehicles, and began to vary their daily travel routines. But both Julie and Michael were deeply dissatisfied with merely reacting to the intimidation by alarm and self-protection.

They soon were able to identify their antagonist as they recognized Trapp's voice through his public appearances. Julie sought direction in Proverbs and other scripture passages that warned against allowing one's life to be consumed by hatred. She wished she could send these passages to the Klansman who had placed them in his cross-hairs.

Michael began calling Trapp to listen to the hate messages on Trapp's own answering machine. Then Michael started to leave brief comments when he called, hoping they might break through the defenses of Trapp's troubled mind. "Why do you hate me?" Michael asked. "You don't even know me, so how can you hate me?"

After a public controversy when Trapp sponsored a white supremacist show, a TV news interview of Trapp showed him with Hitler paraphernalia and wearing his Klan robes. This prompted Michael to call Trapp's phone again. In the message, he reminded Trapp that the first repressive measures the Nazis took were aimed at people just like Trapp, those with physical handicaps. "You would have been among the first to die under Hitler. Why do you love the Nazis so much?"

By this time, many Christians and Jews in Lincoln, Nebraska, knew of Trapp's legendary career in hatred. Some were his medical caregivers, as he frequently unleashed his anger on them, too. Some were his neighbors, recipients of his hate mail and threats. Many resorted to praying that this man, consumed with hatred, might turn from his destructive ways. One former nurse sent Trapp a letter promising healing for his bitterness, hatred, and hurt if he gave his life to God instead of the KKK.

Against all probability, Larry Trapp began to turn! One day he picked up the phone while Michael was leaving one of his prodding messages. At first Trapp responded angrily. But Michael urged Trapp to drop his hatred and consider a chance to find real love. Trapp soon called the Weissers again but this time with cracks of doubt in his brusque manner. Trapp admitted his confusion and illness, and his uncertainty about how to get out of the life he was leading.

Julie was ready for this moment. She had discussed with Michael their plan for how to respond if such a conversation with Trapp ever materialized. Quickly, Michael told Trapp they were bringing him a meal at his home that very evening. Four months after Trapp first accosted them, Michael and Julie offered to enter Trapp's domain. But they did so tentatively. Friends and family warned of an ambush.

When they arrived with carry-out meals for three, they found a remorseful man behind the masks. He spoke of wanting to quit the Klan and turn away from the racist hatred that had consumed him. He asked the Weissers' help in removing the clutter of Nazi materials from his tiny apartment, and for their forgiveness for the cruelty he had inflicted. All three were reduced to tears.

Over a meal of carry-out fried chicken in November 1991, Trapp began a lengthy process of healing his pain-wracked life. He took decisive steps to quit the Ku Klux Klan, renouncing the racism that had made him infamous. He also began calling the people he had harassed in the black community, the wider Jewish community, and others whom he had offended. Some brushed off his apologies, finding it difficult to trust his sudden change from arrogance and bluster to repentance.

Led by the courageous imagination of Cantor Michael and Julie Weisser, a circle of friendship grew up around the former antagonist who had wreaked havoc in so many lives. As Larry Trapp accepted their love and support, he found a peace that had long eluded him. As Trapp's health failed and he required assisted living, the Weissers took him into their already crowded home and gave him food and shelter. Their gift of *shalom* helped Trapp find reconciliation with distant family members after decades of estrangement.

When a religion writer at the *Lincoln Journal Star* broke the story, the editors buried it on an inner page in a Sunday edition.[3] But the power of friendship and love to overcome hatred and fear was more intriguing than the local news staff realized. Soon the Associated Press picked up the story and ran it in 1,500 newspapers and 3,500 radio broadcasts in the United States, plus more than 8,000 outlets in Europe. The Religious News Service and *Time* magazine featured the story as well.

One significant milestone in this story of recovery and reconciliation was the February 1992 celebration of Martin Luther King Jr. day in Lincoln. The same Larry Trapp, who had previously used the occasion to denounce Dr. King in racial epithets plastered around the community, this time joined with members of the NAACP and the wider interfaith council to honor the man who gave his life to racial reconciliation. That year the service was held in the synagogue led by Cantor Michael Weisser.

Within a few months, Larry Trapp had undergone a transformation and was seeking membership in the groups he had formerly targeted with hatred. He petitioned to join the NAACP and, though some objected, overcame the resistance through his sincerity. Trapp also began giving public lectures to expose the inner workings of the secretive hate groups he had known so well. He cooperated with ongoing criminal investigations, which incurred threats of retaliation from his former colleagues in racism across the nation.

Most remarkably, the loving care of the Weissers had awakened in Trapp a new interest in God and in the faith of his rescuers. Trapp studied Judaism and decided to join the congregation led by Michael Weisser. In June 1992, the synagogue officially received him as a convert. Even as his health continued to deteriorate, Trapp found a life he had almost missed entirely, surrounded by friendship, faith, and love.

In September 1992, Larry Trapp's body succumbed to decades of neglecting his diabetes. But his death was not a defeat. For in the teaching of the rabbis, to save a life is to save an entire world. Through the Weissers' example, the world is left to ponder the all-transforming power of love.

9. *AGAPE* DELIVERED UNDER FIRE

When I first met Nikola Škrinjarić in 1993, he had already moved through several careers. For a time he had been a psychic healer, specializing in gangrene-ridden wounds. During another season he had worked as a truck driver in North Africa. By the time war broke out in eastern Croatia where his parents were living, Nikola was driving truck back home in Croatia. He had a tiny apartment in Zagreb, the capital. He was tough, not easily frightened or disturbed.

Yet the strange healing powers that had made Nikola successful and given him acclaim in his community had not brought him real satisfaction in life. "I could get anything I wanted, using those powers," he remembers. But something was missing in his life, and Nikola grew restless.

Along the way, he became acquainted with an elderly Pentecostal pastor. This pastor was experienced in spiritual struggle and had a ministry of deliverance from evil powers. Nikola allowed the pastor to pray for his release from the unseen powers that had bound him. Through the pastor's intervention and prayer, Nikola encountered Jesus. Over six months, Nikola had been transformed into a new person, eager to testify to the liberating power of God's Holy Spirit.

I had returned to the embattled Balkans in 1993, seeking stories of Christians who were confronting the evils of ethnic cleansing, civil war, and genocide. I knew the territory well, having resided in Tito's Yugoslavia for nine relatively calm years before the wars of the 1990s tore the Balkans apart. First in Croatia and then in Bosnia, many friends of mine had been displaced, their villages overrun by rampaging looters. Whole regions of the former Yugoslavia were blockaded and unsafe for civilian travel. Churches lay in ruins and hospitals suffered attacks. Large modern cities were besieged and rivers of refugees streamed away in any direction that offered relief from the horrors they'd experienced in their homes and villages. Some of my former seminary students fled to seek shelter in nearby cities or went abroad for a season. Others stayed on, determined to do what they could to bind up the wounds of war and witness against its horrors.

Nikola's own parents and the rest of his family became refugees, chased out of their Croatian villages in the rapidly escalating violence by marauding bands of Serbs. They headed for relative safety in Zagreb. Nikola took them into his meager bachelor's accommodations. They were angry and mired in despair. How could their former friends and neighbors gang up against them like this? People who had lived side by side for decades suddenly turned on each other in vicious attacks, killing and maiming, seizing houses, and plundering the land.

Nikola began to pray for his parents. He prayed that the power of the gospel that had released him from bondage would also liberate their spirits from the grievous wounds of war. Through his tender, respectful love and modeling, they did, indeed, begin to heal. Nikola introduced them to Jesus and the gospel, making it clear that they could move beyond hatred to new life.

Nikola responded to the devastating war by delivering truckloads of relief supplies for a Christian organization called *Agape*. Churches in Croatia had gathered whatever they could to share with people they had never met in Bosnia. The suffering was immense; some towns and communities were nearing starvation. Driving into the war zone was extremely dangerous, but Nikola was not deterred. He picked his way through hazardous terrain to reach besieged civilian populations in Mostar, the second-largest city in Bosnia.

Agape rented a warehouse in Mostar. Workers sandbagged the warehouse openings against the mortar shells that rained down unpredictably from the forces on the other side. Local Christians distributed food and clothing to the desperate population trapped without escape. After several hazardous journeys into and out of Mostar by truck, Nikola was so moved with compassion that he decided to give himself to the people of Mostar and share their situation directly. He moved to Mostar, and began leading the relief work for *Agape* there.

Nikola also began voicing his hope of the gospel. He spoke of the good news in ways that made sense to people mired in the ethnic-driven civil war and genocide. "If only these people could experience the power of forgiveness in Christ like my own family has," he remembers observing in that early stage, "they would find a totally different approach to life."

The distribution of relief supplies brought crowds of people to the door of the *Agape* warehouse. But for Nikola, it was the intangible relief—the peace of Christ—that he was most eager to share. That peace could come only through reconciliation with God and with neighbor.

Nikola refused to discriminate among recipients when distributing relief goods. Other organizations gave to their own people. But for Nikola, human need was the only criterion for receiving aid.

The community that formed around the *Agape* relief warehouse became a shining example for a life together that had been rendered impossible everywhere else in the region. "Life together" (*suživot*) across ethnic divides had become a slogan for ridicule in the wider society. But in Mostar, under the guns and shells of a tightly divided city, Nikola gathered people of every background into a new fellowship. Precious little fruit had come from decades of evangelical Christian witness up to that point. Now the tangible fruits of reconciliation began to attract new believers.

A significant new round in Nikola's witness came when he invited his fiancée, Sandra, to leave relative safety in Croatia to join him in Mostar. He wanted to marry her in the middle of the war, right there in the midst of the conflict. Their act of courage was a powerful witness to God's presence there. A rousing sermon at the wedding brought even more Mostar residents into the growing fellowship. The new couple started a family there in the war zone, thus giving further testimony to the power of God to embrace hope and a future in the midst of despair.

"Didn't you experience some close calls with gunfire?" I asked Nikola. Oh yes, he reported. He had narrowly escaped a mortar blast that decimated a room just seconds after he had left it. On another occasion, a sniper from the other side of the small river that divided the embattled city took a shot at Nikola. The sniper missed only by a few inches. Nikola smiled, saying, "Something must have disturbed the sniper!"

The small outpost in Mostar, that holy experiment of *suživot*, included people of all the representative backgrounds in Bosnia: Serbs, Croats, Muslim Bošnjaks, Hungarians, Roma, and others. Even after the war ended, Mostar's bright beacon of hope inspired other Christian fellowships. A dozen years later, new multi-ethnic congregations had taken root across the troubled region and helped to bring about a new quality of life following years of hatred and ethnic cleansing. Nikola's courageous legacy led the way for many who dared to be the true custodians of "life together."

10. "STANDING WITH OUR NEIGHBORS"

In a town as small as Harrisonburg, where I live in the Shenandoah Valley of western Virginia, it is not every day that reporters from the world's media descend to cover a court case. But when the BBC from London, Voice of America from Washington, and the Public Broadcasting System all carry the same small-town story, you know you are in an interesting vortex, at least for the moment.

Our community has experienced a significant increase of ethnic diversity, beginning with the period after World War II. It was then that churches in the Valley began helping to resettle refugees from the war's devastation, and that work has continued to the present time. Refugees from America's wars in Southeast Asia added to the local color and, more recently, families fleeing the unrest of the Middle East have found safe harbor among us.

The early trickle of guests welcomed here has become a river. The city of Harrisonburg has the fastest-growing population of English-language learners in the state, rising from 6 percent to 39 percent in 13 years, and with more than 45 native languages spoken in a school system of 4,300 students. Jon Barton, director of the Virginia Council of Churches in Richmond, credits the churches in the Valley with leading and supporting this influx of newcomers, welcoming strangers and diversity even when the general climate in the country is souring toward immigrants.

By the summer of 2006, some 70 families from Iraq's Kurdish population had made their home in Harrisonburg. They came from among 6,000 or so who had been evacuated by the United States after the first Gulf War against Saddam Hussein, first to Turkey, then to Guam. In 1997, when the first families of Kurdish refugees arrived in Virginia, many of them found work in the poultry industry.

Like other refugees, these Kurdish immigrants began to thrive in the local economy. Unemployment rates are low here, thanks to agricultural production and many service jobs. Refugees also found ways to send financial support to family members left behind in Saddam's Iraq. Iraq's failed banking system required relatives in America to transfer funds through intermediaries with accounts in nearby countries such as Turkey. This arrangement, known as *hawala* among various immigrant groups, had become a lifeline for family members who depended on such support with local economies in ruin.

With little notice, however, all *hawala* operations for informal transfer of funds overseas became suspect under the Patriot Act that was passed after the terror attacks of September 11, 2001. Whether the participants knew it or not, their formerly acceptable actions had now become illegal. Prosecutors across the country had arrested 155 people in the four years following the Act's passage, striking fear into many immigrant communities.

Kurdish homes in Harrisonburg were raided by federal agents in August 2004. Arrests followed in October 2005 for four leading men. Even though the government eventually agreed they had no evidence linking the money transfers of these four Kurds to any terrorist activities, the activity itself was deemed illegal and punishable by law. Aid sent to families back home—for medical treatment, funeral expenses, or basic food and supplies—was all illegal. In addition, during the 2004 raid, agents seized funds on hand for a down payment on a house, a sum of $20,000. The money was held almost two years, even though the owner was never charged with a crime.

Harrisonburg's local mosque serves a diverse community of immigrants and others who meet regularly for prayers and worship. Their common language is English with some Arabic added. The Imam is Kakahama Askary, who also teaches at James Madison University in town. He and his American-born wife gathered some friends for tea and conversation about the difficulties facing the vulnerable immigrant population. Like the men on trial, Askary is a Kurd but is also a naturalized U.S. citizen. He had arrived before this more recent group of refugees.

People from Harrisonburg and Rockingham County had previously rallied around the local Muslim community amid the fear and suspicion that followed the September 11, 2001 attacks. Some Muslims had feared going out in public, even to shop for groceries, in the aftermath of that terror. But they discovered that friends and neighbors in their new homeland would stand with them against random retaliatory violence.

But what to do with these mounting legal threats against four Kurdish men arrested for *hawala* activities? An interest group that was meeting informally as a local affiliate of the Fellowship of Reconciliation (FOR) first took up the cause of the four arrested men. FOR is a long-standing movement committed to working for peaceful solutions. The local affiliate group had earlier sponsored a Peace Festival in Harrisonburg that brought together Jews, Muslims, Catholics, and Protestants. Now they formed an action group, Standing With Our Neighbors (SWON), inviting citizens to support the Kurdish community in this harrowing time.

SWON participants helped pay legal fees and wrote letters to the newspaper editor. Even more, they began inviting a wide circle of sympathizers to show their support publicly. The planners drafted a manifesto that garnered more than 600 signatures and appeared as a paid advertisement in the local newspaper. Videographer Jerry Holsopple guided a team who made a brief documentary depicting the life of the local Kurdish community.

A SWON delegation made the two-hour trip to Roanoke, Virginia, to meet with John Brownlee, the zealous U.S. attorney whose Joint Terrorism Task Force persisted in investigating and prosecuting the four Kurds long after ruling out any ties to terrorism. The aggressive investigation involved the FBI, Immigration and Customs, three other federal agencies, and six state and local law enforcement bodies. The delegation's pleas for mercy appeared to have no effect on the aggressive prosecution of the case. They were told that the *hawala* actions, although harmless, were still illegal and must be prosecuted even if the defendants had no ties to terrorism.[4]

After the tedious wait during investigations, Rasheed Qambari was first to be tried. On January 30, 2006, he was found guilty as charged on felony counts under the Patriot Act. Testimony was not permitted on whether or not he knew that his humanitarian activity had suddenly become illegal. The jury spent just 40 minutes deliberating, even though the foreman later commended Qambari's motives as "admirable."

Two of the three other defendants who faced similar charges made a plea agreement and took their chances with the judge on sentencing. The fourth faced a later trial on his own after nearly reaching a plea agreement then finding himself unable to admit guilt when he steadfastly maintained his innocence. Later he, too, pled guilty on reduced charges. But the threat of prison and deportation loomed large for all of them. Sentencing for the first three was set for June 26.

At that point, SWON launched a massive effort to bring as many supporters as possible to the sentencing. The small courtroom allowed only several dozen people to attend the sentencing, but hundreds more rallied outside in a peaceful vigil, lining the sidewalks beside the court. Mennonites, Brethren, Quakers, Catholics, Presbyterians, Methodists, and many others joined in the downtown demonstration.

As demonstrators prayed and carried signs to mark the event, the U.S. district judge said the presence of the supportive crowd is evidence that the defendants had adjusted well to their new homes in this culture and society. Taking the men's solid work records into account and their cooperation with the investigation, he handed down surprisingly lenient sentences compared to the severity of the charges: small fines and a period of probation for each. A month later, the same leniency was shown to the fourth defendant.

That none of the Kurds served prison time was cause for great rejoicing. Mike Medley, who led the SWON efforts, shared with his congregation: "I am deeply encouraged by what we have witnessed of the power of informal community networking among people who have shared goals and values. The amazing results of such networking testify to me of the powerful hand of God coordinating our actions and using them to plant seeds of peace."

Against a national trend of growing hostility toward immigrants and newcomers, small-town Harrisonburg and its religious communities stood tall in their public commitment to hospitality over fear, and to peaceful co-existence rather than paranoia toward their neighbors.

11. A President's Legacy of Peace

I met Macedonia's President Boris Trajkovski in May 2002, when he called upon an international group of ecumenical scholars to hold a religious dialogue in Macedonia in hopes of averting a civil war. The youthful Trajkovski staked his political career on the hope that religion could be mobilized for the good of all his people rather than contributing to the forces that tear a country apart. As a minority Protestant, he was leading a country of majority Orthodox Christians locked in turmoil with a restive Muslim minority.

A small, landlocked country in the southeast corner of Europe, Macedonia was an ancient land forging a new identity in the 1990s after the fall of communism. Its first round of leaders were recycled ex-communists, each one reaching for a new political identity in the grab-bag of pre-communist parties that had existed more than half a century earlier.

How could this little country escape the lethal forces that were ripping nearby Bosnia to shreds? Could its new leadership avoid the conflicts that had created bitter enemies and rivers of refugees in next-door Albania, Kosovo, Croatia, and Serbia? Tito's Yugoslavia was now divided into five successor states. Of the five, only Slovenia and Macedonia had managed to pull themselves together without bloodshed.

This new and ancient land had all the ingredients for another Balkan ethnic cataclysm. Its southern neighbor, Greece, disputed the right to use Macedonia as its name, because Macedonia is also the name of a northern province in Greece. From the north, Serbia's Orthodox Church disputed the independence of the Macedonian Orthodox Church. Slavic Bulgaria from the east contested Macedonia's ethnic and linguistic integrity. They claimed that the majority of Macedonians were Slavic by language and Christian Orthodox by religious heritage, making them essentially Bulgarians.

In addition to all of these external challenges were internal struggles. Macedonia's Albanian Muslim minority, comprising between 25 and 30 percent of the population, had high birthrates and low employment levels, and its Muslim population was demanding more adequate access to education, social services, and political participation.

Macedonia's fledgling democracy had, for the most part, managed to avoid the worst mistakes of the disasters in nearby Albania, Kosovo, and Bosnia. The Macedonians preserved a political system that required inter-ethnic collaboration for success at the polls. No single party could command a majority without alliances that crossed the ethnic divisions between (Christian Orthodox) Macedonians and (Muslim) Albanians. Long after ethnic separatism and partitioning had prevailed in Serbia, Bosnia, and Croatia farther north, Macedonia still had political, military, and police participation from each of its major ethnic communities.

One young leader came to personify the hope that reason, compassion, and cooperation could be the torch to keep Macedonia moving toward a brighter future. Trained in law and with experience in the construction industry, Trajkovski moved quickly through the ranks of the largest opposition party. His facility in English and wide-ranging international contacts equipped him to lead the country's foreign affairs commission from 1995 to 1998. When his party won elections and came to power late in 1998, Trajkovski at 42 years of age became deputy foreign minister. What made this truly remarkable were his family roots in the tiny Protestant minority.

Three months later, Kosovo, next door in southern Serbia, erupted in violence between Orthodox Serbs and Muslim Albanians. NATO entered the fray, bombing Belgrade (Serbia's capital) and the Serb military forces responsible for the "ethnic cleansing" that drove several hundred thousand Albanians from their homes in Kosovo. Waves of angry, desperate Albanian refugees flooded into Macedonia, taking shelter among the already impoverished Albanians there. Trajkovski became the point-person between his government and the international community, arguing passionately and effectively for extending hospitality in this humanitarian disaster. He secured substantial international assistance. Macedonia provided for over 360,000 Albanian refugees from Kosovo during a time when Macedonia's own resources were already stressed.

Later in 1999, his party put Trajkovski forward as a candidate for the presidential elections. Having earned respect as a tough negotiator in the international community and as a moderate at home who could bridge the interests of the Macedonian communities, he won a surprise victory in a hotly contested race. Analysts agree that the moderate Albanian vote gave him the margin of victory.

The toughest test came two years after the Kosovo eruption. Thousands of aggrieved Kosovar Albanian refugees who flooded into Macedonia's towns enflamed the already restless Macedonian Albanians. Battle-tested militia leaders from Kosovo began recruiting among Macedonian Albanian youth, using weapons and tactics imported from insurgencies elsewhere. Suddenly, Macedonia faced an armed uprising in February 2001 that quickly gained control over 17 percent of Macedonia's territory.

This situation easily might have triggered a military response. The Macedonian government could have mobilized its forces to defeat the insurgents. As the country teetered on the brink of all-out civil war, the president's support among moderates eroded. Yet, as he told one advisor, "How can I order a battle in which I know many will die when I am pledged to promote peace? My very faith goes against this." To a British reporter, he declared, "Better to talk for 1,000 days than to fight for one."

Against many objections, even from his own party's prime minister and his parliamentary counterparts, Trajkovski convened a lengthy set of negotiations among the four leading parties, two each from the Macedonian and the Albanian sides. These negotiations were held in Ohrid, an ancient city on a lake that symbolizes the deep cultural heritage of Macedonia. Trajkovski met the insurgents' concerns on his own terms, taking their demands for group rights to a higher level by stressing individual rights and responsibilities. He consistently framed the discussion toward the future, with security and prosperity for all citizens based on trust and cooperation. Putting his own integrity on the line, he modeled a spirit of service and humility. He persisted in the negotiations until a Framework Agreement was reached and ratified by a dubious parliament. The Agreement called for international assistance in disarming the insurgents, and increased political participation and inclusion for all ethnic groups.

Trajkovski's efforts drew criticism from hardliners on all sides. Even so, he consolidated his gains by a host of domestic and international successes. He shored up external alliances and cooperation, and built trust and promoted the rule of law in a civil society with a robust and growing free-market economy. He was an early advocate and promoter of technology. His legacy includes giving Macedonia technological distinction as the first country to offer broadband access in all its territory. He leveraged that achievement from a system installed in local elementary schools.

Trajkovski tirelessly pursued his goals for Macedonia's integration through wider European prospects and membership in NATO's security provisions. He reached out to cooperate with his regional neighbors, Albania and Croatia. By all accounts, his Christian faith seemed to provide an explicit source of strength and comfort, even when his positions were mistrusted or misunderstood.

President Trajkovski once gave an interview to a sympathetic journalist while a noisy anti-NATO demonstration played out under his window in the parliament building. He expressed his determination to continue working for Macedonia's well-being despite opposition from others who objected to his negotiations with internal Albanian rebels. He cited Egypt's president, Anwar Sadat, who had flown to Israel to meet his Israeli counterparts, even though the two countries recently had been at war and had no diplomatic relations. Trajkovski remembered how Sadat defended his move, saying, "I am going to these talks for peace. I am going to bring peace and prosperity for my people." Trajkovski insisted he was doing the very same thing. "I want to bring peace and prosperity to all the citizens of Macedonia. This is my vision".[5]

When Trajkovski convened Macedonia's religious communities for improved trust and cooperation in 2002, I was one of the international guests in Skopje, the capital of Macedonia. On that occasion, he invited representatives from the predominant Orthodox Christian community; the Islamic community; and representatives of the Catholic, Protestant, and Jewish communities to confer with each other.

The participants reached new agreements for regularly scheduled interfaith meetings at the top levels and created a Council of Interreligious Cooperation. Direct interaction between the top two theological faculties—Orthodox and Islamic—helped to foster respect among those training new religious leaders. In a country where atheism had been the ruling ideology just a decade before and where mutual suspicions ran rife, these commitments paved new ground and held much promise for the future.

Boris Trajkovski's own father had been imprisoned for his faith soon after the communists took power in the wake of World War II. Forced into hard labor, he was assigned to work on a luxurious villa on the mountain that overlooks Skopje. Later it became the home of Macedonia's presidents. Boris Trajkovski occupied the residence for a little more than four years as an innovative, courageous, peacebuilding president. Sadly, he died in a tragic plane crash in February 2004 on his way to an international conference on development aid for Macedonia. He was only 47, but his peaceful legacy continues.

This period of Macedonia's history perhaps would be more notorious if it had conceded to violence, as nearby Bosnia and Kosovo had. But the basic decency and leadership of President Boris Trajkovski deserves a celebrated place in history. His legacy of resisting the tide of suspicion and mistrust stands as a model for his successors. His devotion to peace with justice for all Macedonia's citizens spared the world from yet another Balkan bloodbath.

12. Mennonite Farmers Break a Boycott

Two generations after the events in this story transpired, it has slipped from the collective memory of the community where it occurred. But it's too good to remain hidden: An anonymous Mennonite farmer in Norfolk, Virginia, stood up to the Ku Klux Klan on behalf of a Jewish merchant. My Serbian friend, Stevan Madjarac, heard this story on National Public Radio in Iowa where he lives. He notified his Mennonite friends in Pennsylvania and Virginia about the story, and added his own word of gratitude. He said the story reminded him of Mennonite farmers who had helped him during his family's journey out of a labyrinth of ethnic violence in Croatia.

Stevan was born in a Marxist home in a Serbian village in rural Croatia. While he was serving his required military term in another region of Tito's Yugoslavia in the 1970s, a local Baptist family befriended him and led him to Christ. When he returned to his home in Croatia, Stevan faced multiple challenges as a minority Serb in a season of rising Croatian separatist nationalism. Even among the minority Serbs, those who got ahead had hitched their fate to the Communist party.

Stevan studied agriculture at the university and became an expert on soybeans. He researched and advocated innovative practices with farmers in all regions of the country. While the Yugoslav communist system still held together, his keen entrepreneurial spirit found plenty of opportunities to improve life for his fellow citizens. Though many regarded him suspiciously for his active Christian faith, his beliefs did not compromise his success as it might have in other professions.

Stevan's and my paths crossed when our two families shared a household in Zagreb, Croatia, during the later years of communist rule in Yugoslavia, from 1987 to 1989. Stevan's young family and ours did some urban gardening together. He delighted in experimenting with sweet corn and other seeds we brought from the States. We participated in church ministry together as we related to many young adults in the university world.

The growing suspicions toward his faith and the separatist political passions in Croatia, however, began to erode Stevan's confidence in his future. Whether because of his Christian faith or his minority Serbian ethnic status, he faced tougher and tougher employment prospects as the economy began to fail. Eager to provide for his young family, he looked to international firms for employment.

Eventually, a Mennonite network gave Stevan a strong recommendation for a position based in Austria with the Pioneer seed company. That connection was made via a Pioneer agent, Wilmer Nissley, who attended a rural Pennsylvania congregation, Erisman Mennonite, which had been supporting my family's work in Yugoslavia. For several years, Stevan and his family found shelter and solid employment with Pioneer in neighboring Austria. Meanwhile, things had become desperate in rural Croatia as the Serbian minority communities were plunged into the darkest chapters of civil war. Many from Stevan's family and other nearby Serbian villages fled their homes.

Pioneer eventually moved Stevan and his family to Iowa, where for more than a decade they thrived among the cornfields of that lush land. At one point they sojourned in southeastern Virginia while Stevan pursued graduate studies on a generous scholarship. There they attended a local Mennonite congregation.

Years passed. Then one morning an email from Stevan tied together rural Pennsylvania, Virginia, and the flatlands of Iowa. He wanted to know whether we had heard National Public Radio's "Stories of Good Deeds" that day.[6] The story featured heroics by unnamed and forgotten Mennonite farmers who had made the crucial difference for a hardware store owner in Norfolk, Virginia, during the 1930s. The owner, Mr. Gordon, was a Jewish immigrant merchant who was being boycotted by the local Ku Klux Klan.

As reported to NPR in 2003 by Mr. Gordon's grandson, one Mennonite farmer came into the store and inquired about the owner's difficulties. Hearing of this ethnic discrimination, the farmer apparently left and spread the word among others in his community. Soon a steady stream of Mennonite farmers brought that season's business to Mr. Gordon to break the boycott and assure his survival in business. More than six decades later, the family business has changed through several forms but it still provides employment to Mr. Gordon's grateful grandson.

In southern Virginia, this triumph of economic justice seems to have slipped from the collective memory of those Mennonite farmers' descendents. A quick round of inquiry failed to turn up any recollection of the incident among Mennonites there.

While it's nice, of course, to be recognized for acts of faithful response to injustice, the story resonated with Stevan for different reasons. He wrote with delight about this story to his Mennonite friends in Pennsylvania and Virginia:

> Today I listened to this report on NPR's *Morning Edition*. It was quite a story! We have such a great memory of your church and just wanted to share the story with you in memory of those farmers who, though anonymous, made a great contribution to the cause of Christ. If you get a chance, could you do me a favor and share this story with others in your congregation who still might remember us?
> Blessings,
> Stevan

13. A Surprising Forgiveness

It seemed the whole world was electrified by a new and tragic story. Another school shooting. Another community torn by grief and pain. Another tormented gunman, brandishing weapons and inexplicable hostility, unleashing his madness on innocent victims. Another collective gasp and the brief pause to ask ourselves: What kind of society are we becoming?

But this story would follow a remarkably different course.

It was October 2, 2006 when horror shattered the quiet rural community of Nickel Mines in southeastern Pennsylvania. A 32-year-old truck driver named Charles Roberts walked into an Amish one-room schoolhouse. He expelled the boys and several adult women, including the 20-year-old teacher. He took 10 schoolgirls as hostages and prepared for a lengthy siege. Judging from the equipment he brought into the school, he apparently intended to torture and sexually molest the girls.

An all too familiar scene of school-yard terror unfolded. Those who escaped headed for a nearby farm to call 911, and law enforcement officials responded promptly. After a brief standoff, Roberts began shooting. Within a half hour, five of his victims and Roberts himself were dead or mortally wounded. Another five schoolgirls were gravely wounded but would survive.

Up to that point, the story was tragically similar to a series of schoolhouse rampages in recent U.S. history. The public record enumerates almost 40 separate incidents of gun-related casualties in schools since the shootings at the University of Texas at Austin in 1966. Among the most notorious was the killing spree at Columbine High School in Colorado in 1999.

In most cases, some explanation eventually emerges for the perpetrator's actions. The alienated killer holds a grievance toward those he attacks. Some are targets of bullying, bent on settling the score with students or teachers. What was so confounding in this schoolhouse shooting, however, was that no apparent connection existed between Roberts and his chosen victims. Why Roberts would single out innocent Amish girls for slaughter defied explanation.

The Amish are a faith community whose members generally avoid the spotlight of public attention. By their own choice, they remain relatively secluded from the rest of the world. Also by choice, they avoid many of the trappings and conveniences of modern society. They choose to live quietly and peaceably, refusing to bear weapons, join the military, or even the local police force. Many do serve with local firefighting units.

The Amish preserve patterns of peasant farming communities from bygone generations. Their separateness and simplicity ironically bring millions of "worldly" tourists to their doorstep. The tourists spend millions of dollars each year to observe the Amish cultivating their rich, beautiful fields and to buy their handcrafted quilts and furniture.

And so, as horrendous as school shootings are, the shock waves of this violent intrusion felt like a tsunami. It seemed like a vicious strike at the heart of innocence personified by these gentle people. As the earliest version of this story was hitting the news, the world was stunned to witness the forgiving character of this quaint Christian community. These peaceable people would transform the vicious violation of their innocent children into a story even more remarkable.

Under the glare of invasive cameras and a gawking world, the Amish Christians of Nickel Mines handled the tragedy the same way they had dealt with other hard times: by banding together and sharing comfort in an outpouring of quiet care and mutual grief. They streamed by the hundreds to the victims' neighboring farms, bearing food for the gatherings. Funerals hosted in their homes (there are no church buildings set apart for sacred use) would unfold over the next several days.

In their earliest conversations with the media, members of the Amish community were already speaking of forgiveness. In subsequent hours and days, what transformed this story from "just another school shooting" was the Amish community's ready and unrehearsed generosity toward the family of Charles Roberts. Away from cameras, the Amish reached out to Roberts' widow and children, even his parents and grandparents, all living within a short distance of the schoolhouse. Relatives of the grieving families visited Roberts' widow and followed up numerous times over the next few days. The parents of the slain girls invited Roberts' family members to attend their daughters' funerals. Amish representatives also attended Roberts' funeral and expressed their condolences and forgiveness to his widow.

The Amish community sought to reinforce their forgiveness and goodwill in tangible ways. As gifts to help with the victims' medical costs and recovery efforts poured in from around the world, the Amish and their local supporters formed a public unit, the Nickel Mines Accountability Committee, to manage the funds for the victims' needs. In their earliest consideration of victims, they included the Roberts family, designating a portion of the funds for his widow and children.

This generosity astonished the global audience and confirmed that this story of school violence was different from every other. The victims' grieving families were determined to resist their natural impulses of hatred and revenge. They refused to allow the bitter fruits of a tormented killer to multiply in widening circles of retaliation. Rather, the Amish chose the way of forgiveness.

Why did they take these surprising actions? And why are the rest of us so shocked at their generous response? Why does the practice of forgiveness seem so foreign, even to many Christians?

The Amish would want us to understand that they were acting out of obedience to the teachings of Jesus and the earliest Christians: Forgive others as you have been forgiven. Do not repay evil with evil, but repay evil with good. The Amish see generous forgiveness as basic to Christian faith, not as a unique aspect of their Amish tradition. Despite their distinctive appearance and practices, they do not regard themselves as outside the mainstream of Christian teachings. Although they pay little attention to theological developments among the larger Christian traditions, their own adherence to Jesus' teachings is something they would expect other Christians to recognize and affirm. They might ask us, Isn't forgiveness a practice that Jesus asks all Christians to follow?

The compelling simplicity of the Amish response to this tragedy didn't diminish the evil that they suffered. Their grief and pain were immense. But their beautiful acts of forgiveness eclipsed the killer's horrendous deeds. What transformed this story was their ready generosity toward the killer's family and their insistence on treating the Roberts family as real human beings, hurting people who themselves needed healing.

I am not inclined to romanticize the Amish way of life in their resistance to social and cultural change. Those who know the Amish communities better than I do assure us that the Amish have blemishes and faults like the rest of us. But the Amish have certainly earned the right to be heard as witnesses to an alternative way of life with their sturdy refusal to return evil for evil. They paid the price of extreme suffering without retaliation. It seems our own surprise at their actions reveals more about us than about them.

Some of the outpouring of sympathy from around the world came in direct response to help the Amish previously had given to others. The Amish community's generosity came full circle, from victims of Hurricane Katrina who received assistance from Amish carpenters, and from my personal friends in Serbia who had received Amish gifts of food and relief after the Balkan wars of the 1990s.

Amish leaders expressed a hope that their witness would encourage others who suffer. This hope was fulfilled in part during the memorial for victims of the Virginia Tech shootings that killed 33 in April 2007. Virginia Governor Tim Kaine cited the Amish response when he urged forgiveness and healing after the shooting spree. Officials from the Virginia campus were invited to the Nickel Mines community in October 2007 in a gesture of solidarity for the community's one-year commemoration of the schoolhouse shootings.

This story was transformed into a triumph of forgiveness. The Amish response out of obedience to Jesus had turned the spotlight away from the terror its perpetrator intended and focused it instead on the amazing capacity to heal and forgive. The Amish reminded a watching world that it is possible to rise above the destructive cycle of violent retaliation. It is possible to recover the goodness of God's *shalom.*

14. GIVING LIFE

It's November 2005. Israeli soldiers raid a refugee camp inside the small Palestinian city of Jenin, in the northern part of the West Bank occupied territories. The soldiers had been there before. This time, they shoot a young boy holding a toy gun. This, too, has happened before. Twelve-year-old Ahmed Khatib dies, as have many children before and after him.

Since spending a sabbatical semester in the Middle East, these stories are to me more than simply news. Each one has a location, a color, and a smell, with most of them sounding like despair. I have visited the near permanent refugee camps in which successive generations have endured the injustices of limited access to health care, education, and jobs.

But this story of Ahmed in Jenin is more than a blip in this stream of predictable news. Ahmed's parents, in an act of peaceful resistance and anger, chose to donate his organs to save other lives. Within hours of his death in an Israeli hospital, Ahmed's heart, kidneys, liver, and lungs were restoring life to six other people. And his parents, knowing these gifts of life might well go to their "enemies" on the Israeli side of the wall, decided to make the donation without restriction.

Shot in the back of the head, Ahmed had no real chance of surviving after the bullet exploded into deadly fragments. He had been playing a dangerous game.

In the bleak world of the refugee camp, pestering soldiers on raids is one of the few entertainments available to kids. Ahmed's mother, Abla Khatib, candidly acknowledged that her son used to throw stones at the soldiers. The kids lived in a partisan world and regarded the armed fighters on the Palestinian side as their heroes. Those armed fighters were the usual targets of the raiding Israeli soldiers. Ahmed had collected posters of death notices for the Palestinian "martyrs," 59 of whom had been killed just blocks from his home in a fierce attack three years earlier.[7]

The day Ahmed was shot should have been a special day. It was the first day of Eid el-Fitr, the close of Ramadan's month-long fasting typically celebrated with numerous festivities. Ahmed had new clothes for the occasion, and he arose before dawn to help his mother with preparations. He left for the mosque just after daybreak, passing along the graveyard where his heroes, the "martyrs" of the *intifada* (armed resistance to the occupation), were buried. But when word of the soldiers' arrival on yet another raid spread through the streets, Ahmed and many other youngsters swarmed into action. His parents say he did not own a toy gun, for they knew that would be dangerous. But he must have found one in that moment. And the toy he grabbed made him a target.

How deeply must parents reach for the courage to turn such a tragedy into a peace-seeking protest? Ahmed's father, Ismail, knew suffering firsthand. He had lost a brother to kidney failure two decades earlier after a lengthy struggle, in spite of Ismail regularly donating blood for him. Had this and other hardships of living under the Israeli occupation deepened their compassion for others' suffering? Or perhaps the parents' compassion sprung from encountering people awaiting organ transplants while Ahmed lived out his final days on life support in an Israeli hospital.

The decision to give their son's organs to help others didn't come easily. Ismail consulted with his local religious authorities to check whether Islamic law permitted such practices and received clear affirmation from Jenin's *mufti*. Even the resistance fighters in the refugee camp (the al-Aqsa Martyrs' Brigades, locally led by Zakaria Zubeidi) gave tacit approval. As the parents proceeded through the steps of organ donation, they made no attempt to place restrictions on who might receive their son's organs. And at each level, the religious officials and the community affirmed the parents' actions and desire to make this positive statement.

With the painful end of Ahmed's life, six others received hope for a renewed life. Ahmed's heart was given to a 12-year-old Israeli Arab girl. His lungs went to a Jewish teenager with cystic fibrosis. One kidney went to a three-year-old Jewish girl and another to a five-year-old Bedouin Arab. Ahmed's liver was divided between a seven-month-old Jewish girl and an older Jewish mother with hepatitis.

This act of selfless generosity from this tragic event profoundly impacted many, in addition to the six individuals who received a new chance at life. A flurry of news coverage widely reported the surprising story, and leading Israeli politicians, including then Deputy Prime Minister Ehud Olmert, called to apologize to the parents for the shooting death of their son.

One news story reported that Ismail's decision was rooted, in part, in his own earlier experiences working in Israel as a mechanic.[8] His interactions enabled him to distinguish between actions taken by Israel's government and the deeds or attitudes of ordinary Israelis as human beings. The confidence to make such a distinction grew out of basic human interactions that had taken place in better times.

The high concrete wall, called a "separation barrier" by the Israeli government, was then under construction around Jenin. It has now been extended almost the entire length of the country. Unlike his father, 12-year-old Ahmed knew Israelis only as soldiers. His father lamented, "This does not help us. Seeing each other as human beings helps us."[9]

Ahmed's mother, Abla, gave this perspective: "To give away his organs was a different kind of resistance. Violence against violence is worthless. Maybe this will reach the ears of the whole world so they can distinguish between just and unjust. Maybe the Israelis will think of us differently. Maybe just one Israeli will decide not to shoot."[10]

Ahmed's father, Ismail, adds, "The hope is that those people will learn the lesson from what I have done. Those six people will learn the lesson that we are human beings; their families, even if they were serving in the army, will consider what I have done."[11]

15. CONCLUSION:
TOO MUCH GOOD NEWS TO BOG DOWN IN BAD

When I first set out to assemble this collection of stories, I knew that narrowing my selection would be difficult. I had collected over the years a "grab bag" of stories that had moved me, sometimes to tears. Tears, in fact, were a marker for the stories that simply had to be preserved. There are many other footprints worth marking, other heroes of hope whose deeds show us the way:

- Phyllis and Orlando Rodriguez lost their son, Greg, in the September 11, 2001 attacks on the World Trade Center in New York City. Four days after the attacks, sensing the United States would retaliate militarily, they wrote to President Bush and to the *New York Times* to object to any action that would produce suffering and death for many more people. They wrote that military strikes "will not avenge our son's death. Not in our son's name. Our son died a victim of an inhuman ideology. Our actions should not serve the same purpose. Let us grieve. Let us reflect and pray. Let us think about a rational response that brings real peace and justice to our world. But let us not as a nation add to the inhumanity of our times."

• Hundreds of bereaved families in Israel and Palestine have lost loved ones in the Arab/Israeli conflict. Roni Hirschenson lost his 19-year-old son to a suicide bomber in 1995, and another son to suicide after learning that his best friend was killed in a bombing. Roni joins 500 people who have come together through Parents' Circle, a non-governmental organization working for peace that includes both Israeli and Palestinian bereaved parents. When the two sides' respective political leaders stopped talking, this group opened a simple phone line for people on both sides to speak to each other. More than 400,000 calls were placed during the line's first 18 months in service. Hirschenson believes the bereaved can use their status as heroes in their societies to demonstrate the cost of violence and the benefits of peace.

• In another series of unlikely encounters, Arabs and Jews from the Middle East came together in what Israeli writer Yossi Klein Halevi aptly called a "mutually subversive journey."[12] The initiative came from an Arab Christian priest in Nazareth, Father Emil Shufani. He gathered 260 Arabs and

Israeli Jews for a shared journey in May 2003 to Auschwitz, the Nazi death camp in Poland, after months of intensive preparation. Halevi observed that the participants experienced a deeper transformation of self than debates about political and historical perspectives can provide. The journey to Auschwitz was followed by another joint pilgrimage into the heart of Arab culture and civilizations.

- In London, one year after her son was killed in the July 7, 2005 bus and subway bombings, Marie Fatayi Williams announced that she was forgiving her son's killer and leaving all judgment to God: "If I hold onto vengeance, that will continue the suffering." She launched a foundation for peace and conflict resolution named in honor of her son.

- At a conference in Sweden, I met an Israeli peacemaker named Eliyahu McLean. It was his imaginative idea to place banners of protest on the infamous apartheid wall now dividing Israel and the West Bank. The banners depict faces with ridiculous expressions designed to expose the inherent contradiction of the inhumane barrier. Eliyahu is an interfaith bridge builder, a reconciler in constant motion to cross the divides and bring people together in the strength of their religious faith, their humanity, and their ability to laugh, even in the face of despair.

Through the gift of stories, our deepest humanity is stirred when we recognize ourselves in the responses of others. What is the thread that weaves throughout this collection? Again and again, a deed arises out of the creative imagination of people who see despair and yet, in their largeness of spirit, move toward freedom and hope.

As a teacher and promoter of peace and justice, I am sobered to recognize that many of the events recounted in this collection did not begin with an explicit pacifist commitment or conviction. The actors in these dramas generally didn't find their inspiration in classrooms or books. They hadn't rehearsed a philosophical position on violence or sought out opportunities to intervene in tough, ethical issues.

The impetus for their actions resulted from staying alert to the inherent human impulse toward fear and retaliation, grasping how self-defeating that impulse truly is, and then finding a more creative response. These individuals recognized the humanity of the other, perhaps born of their own familiarity with grief and suffering.

These stories help us imagine how we, too, might carry light into the dark corners of our world and subvert vengeance with kindness. Almost all of these accounts depend on ordinary human beings confronting violence and hatred with imagination, courage, and love. In their stories, we ask ourselves whether we can handle the direct implications of our own convictions. Will we dare to live what we believe? Can we ground the hope we proclaim in real deeds? Can we encourage each other in the beautiful and tender art of peacecraft? These stories all say *Yes!* We can break through to live the hope—to see hope personified in deeds. Hope indeed!

DISCUSSION QUESTIONS

Chapter 1: Crazy Like Jesus
1. What does it really mean to be "crazy like Jesus"?
2. In places where conscientious objection to war is prohibited, what should Christians do when faced with conscription?
3. How can Christians support those who wish to stand for peace, even amid opposition?

Chapter 2: Turning Enemies into Friends
1. How should Christians respond when threatened with violence?
2. How do crimes committed against individuals affect the whole community?
3. What are some effective methods that people can use to turn enemies into friends?

Chapter 3: A Franciscan in the Fray
1. How can we help promote reconciliation among different ethnic or racial groups in our own communities?
2. Why do people sometimes turn against their neighbors when faced with upheaval in the community?
3. Who are some people or groups that promote reconciliation in war zones? What makes them effective?

Chapter 4: Moving Toward the Trouble
1. How are some of our country's public institutions racist or divisive?
2. What are some social elements that foster hidden rage in troubled places?
3. How can we find a level of activism that reflects our pacifist beliefs in relation to the risks involved in a potentially volatile situation?

Chapter 5: Sheltering Fallen Tyrants

1. How can we help defuse the climate of fear sometimes present in society?
2. What are some of the moral dilemmas facing those who offer refuge to those who have persecuted them?
3. How did Jesus model the kind of forgiveness and compassion embodied by the German pastor in this story?

Chapter 6: A Protest in Generosity

1. Is it possible to strike a balance between a peace-loving faith and patriotic fervor?
2. What are some creative solutions we can use to reconcile a devotion to nonviolence with the patriotism expressed in today's society?
3. Is it ever right for people who believe in peacemaking to profit from activities that might be seen as promoting various forms of violence?

Chapter 7: Peacemaking on an International Order

1. How can individuals help promote peace when it takes a nation-state to wage war?
2. What are some ways that Christians can help promote peacemaking methods such as Track Two diplomacy?
3. How can a Christian peace witness be convincing to groups that oppose religious faith?

Chapter 8: From Klan to Kin

1. Racist organizations often base their stances on their interpretation of Christianity or another faith. How can we respond to this co-opting of the non-violent Christ?
2. If we or those we know are threatened with violence, how can we respond and still remain faithful to nonviolence?
3. How can we use our faith and the power of love to help transform those whose beliefs oppose ours?

Chapter 9: *Agape* Delivered Under Fire

1. How does the Holy Spirit help liberate us from hatred and other unseen powers of destruction?
2. What are some ways relief agencies can help promote peacemaking?
3. How can we see the power of God intervening to prevent danger or offer protection in our own lives? How has this intervention transformed us?

Chapter 10: "Standing with Our Neighbors"

1. When new ethnic groups arrive in our communities, how can we best welcome them?
2. How can we respond when we believe the laws of our states or nation discriminate against ethnic minorities?
3. How can each of us stand in support of ethnic minorities, especially when they are being threatened or victimized because of government policies or public events such as the Sept. 11, 2001, terrorist attacks?

Chapter 11: A President's Legacy of Peace

1. How can we as Christians respond when other Christians, such as those in Serbia, are involved in violent "ethnic cleansing" or other genocidal practices?
2. For a Christian, can diplomacy ever fail to such an extent that violence, such as a military attack, can be justified?
3. Can the example of one person resisting violence truly effect meaningful change among others in a divided society?

Chapter 12: Mennonite Farmers Break a Boycott

1. Are the members of peace churches such as the Mennonite church always called to stand against racism and other prejudice?
2. What does the gospel say about discriminating against or persecuting those of other ethnic or racial backgrounds?

3. Some Mennonites believe they are not called to activism but to lives of quietude, while others believe they are compelled to seek social change. What does the gospel say about this?

Chapter 13: A Surprising Forgiveness

1. What does it take for a community, much less individuals, to respond with forgiveness following a tragedy such as the Amish school shootings of 2006?
2. Does the example of Amish forgiveness, as it was portrayed in the media, seem too simplistic or deny the reality of grief and mourning?
3. Why were so many people shocked by the public statements of forgiveness made by the Amish after the school shootings? What does this disbelief say about our society?

Chapter 14: Giving Life

1. What are some ways that tragedy can be turned into an opportunity for peaceful activism?
2. Discuss situations in which acts of generosity, such as donating organs, even to one's perceived enemies, can bring about change amid grave turmoil.
3. What does the gospel say about generosity to others, and about putting restrictions on our generous acts?

Conclusion: Too Much Good News to Bog Down in Bad

1. How can those who are victims of violence or their survivors use their experiences to inspire openness and peacemaking among others?
2. Why is it so important for people of faith to forgive when they are victims of violence and leave any judgments to God?
3. How do stories of forgiveness and mercy stir our humanity and cause us to seek peaceful responses to violence?

RESOURCES FOR FURTHER STUDY

For more on **"Crazy Like Jesus,"** see the interview with young Lazar and his pastor, Alexander, in *Beyond the News: Hope for Bosnia*, published by Mennonite Media in VHS format in 1993. The video is available for purchase at www.mennolink.org or check your local library.

For more on **"A Franciscan in the Fray,"** see expanded accounts of the Face to Face Interreligious Service and the Pontanima choir based in Sarajevo, Bosnia, at http://www.pontanima.ba/pontanima.html.

Traces of **"Sheltering Fallen Tyrants"** surfaced in various sermons and reflections, especially in Lutheran circles. The basic outline of Pastor Holmer's story is available online at several sites. For ongoing overview of the changing situation with religious communities in former communist lands, see the journal, *Religion in Eastern Europe*, with multiple years archived at http://ree.georgefox.edu.

"**From Klan to Kin**" draws on the excellent book by Kathryn Watterson, *Not By the Sword* (Simon & Schuster, 1995). The story appeared in many places, but this book gives the fullest treatment.

For more on "*Agape* **Delivered Under Fire**," see the video interview in *Beyond the News: Hope for Bosnia*, published by Mennonite Media in VHS format in 1993. The video is available for purchase at www.mennolink.org or check your local library.

The story in "**A Surprising Forgiveness**" is well documented in an early response by noted Mennonite author and historian, John Ruth, in *Amish Forgiveness* (Herald Press, 2007). An extended reflection is provided by Don Kraybill, Steve Nolt, and David Weaver-Zercher in their work, *Amish Grace* (Jossey-Bass, 2007).

The best account of "**Giving Life**" is found in a sensitive treatment by Chris McGreal in "Ahmed's Gift of Life," *The Guardian*, November 11, 2005.

ENDNOTES

1. For more on this exchange, see Christine Mallouhi, "A Christian in the Sultan's Camp," in *Waging Peace on Islam*. Westmont, Ill.: InterVarsity Press, 2002.

2. Simon & Schuster, 1995.

3. See C.J. Schepers, "Grand Dragon Quits, Takes Jew as Friend," (November 24, 1991).

4. For more on the delegation's efforts, see Jeremy Nafziger, "Homeland Security," *Eighty-One* (June 2006).

5. See "Man of Vision: Interview with Macedonian President Boris Trajkovski," *Central Europe Review*, no. 24 (2001). Or see www.ce-review.org/01/26/vaknin26.html.

6. The NPR story aired on *Morning Edition* on January 27, 2003.

7. See the extensive article by Chris McGreal, "Ahmed's Gift of Life," in *The Guardian* (November 11, 2005). See http://www.guardian.co.uk/world/2005/nov/11/israel1.

8. Ibid.

9. Ibid.

10. Ibid.

11. Ibid.

12. See the *Jerusalem Post*, July 17, 2003. Or see *Jews for Justice for Palestine* at http://www.jfjfp.org/news25/25auschwitz.htm.

About the Author

N. Gerald Shenk has devoted his life to studying the dynamics of religion and social conflict, and promoting paths that lead to peace. He lived and taught for nine years as a young adult in the former Yugoslavia (1977-83, 1986-89), and partnered with local Christians after the break-up of the communist order created turmoil and ethnic warfare in the Balkans (1990-95).

Shenk's work with peacemakers in the former Yugoslavia gave him a deep respect for the courage it takes to face down fears while moving to help heal the wounds of war. His 2003 sabbatical in Jerusalem gave him further insights into the complexities of dealing with deep religious tensions while praying for and pursuing true peace with justice. He participated in a theological conference in Iran in September 2006, and later that month also met the Iranian President in New York City with a religious delegation.

Shenk writes and teaches on themes of Christian peacemaking, social transformation, and religious pluralism.

Since 1989, he teaches at Eastern Mennonite Seminary in Virginia, and also returns to teach in Croatia at the Evangelical Theological Seminary. He holds a Ph.D. from Northwestern University.

METHOD OF PAYMENT

❏ Check or Money Order
(payable to **Good Books** *in U.S. funds)*

❏ Please charge my:

    ❏ MasterCard   ❏ Visa
    ❏ Discover   ❏ American Express

\# _____

exp. date _____

Signature _____

Name _____

Address _____

City _____

State _____

Zip _____

Phone _____

Email _____

SHIP TO: (if different)

Name _____

Address _____

City _____

State _____

Zip _____

Mail order to: **Good Books**
P.O. Box 419 • Intercourse, PA 17534-0419
Call toll-free: 800/762-7171
Fax toll-free: 888/768-3433
Prices subject to change.

Group Discounts for

HOPE INDEED!

ORDER FORM

If you would like to order multiple copies of
Hope Indeed! by N. Gerald Shenk for groups you
know or are a part of, use this form. (Discounts
apply only for more than one copy.)
   Photocopy this page as often as you like.

The following discounts apply:

1 copy	$9.95
2-5 copies	$8.96 each (a 10% discount)
6-10 copies	$8.46 each (a 15% discount)
11-20 copies	$7.96 each (a 20% discount)
21-99 copies	$6.97 each (a 30% discount)
100 or more	$5.97 each (a 40% discount)

Prices subject to change.

Quantity   *Price*   *Total*

_____ copies of *Hope Indeed!* @   _____ _____

PA residents add 6% sales tax _____

Shipping & Handling
(add 10%; $3.00 minimum) _____

TOTAL _____